THE PROMISE
OF DESTINY

1. Louisa May Alcott, 1883. From Ednah D. Cheney, editor, *Louisa May Alcott: Her Life, Letters and Journals.*

THE PROMISE
OF DESTINY

*Children and Women
in the Short Stories
of Louisa May Alcott*

Joy A. Marsella

Contributions to the Study of Childhood and Youth, Number 2

GREENWOOD PRESS
Westport, Connecticut • London, England

PS 1018
M 33
1983

Marsella, Joy A.
   The promise of destiny.

   (Contributions to the study of childhood and youth,
ISSN 0273-124X ; no. 2)
   Bibliography: p.
   Includes index.
   1. Alcott, Louisa May, 1832-1888—Characters—Children.
2. Alcott, Louisa May, 1832-1888—Characters—Women.
3. Children in literature. 4. Women in literature.
I. Title   II. Series.
PS1018.M33 1983   813'.4   82-15573
ISBN: 0-313-23603-8 (lib. bdg.)

Library of Congress Catalog Card Number: 82-15573
ISBN: 0-313-23603-8
ISSN: 0273-124X

First published in 1983

Greenwood Press
A division of Congressional Information Service, Inc.
88 Post Road West
Westport, Connecticut 06881

Printed in the United States of America

10 9 8 7 6 5 4 3 2 1

To my husband, Tony, and my daughters, Laura and Gianna, for their continual support and loving encouragement at all stages of this endeavor.

Contents

Illustrations

Note On Citations

In order to show how Alcott's writing is consistent with both her editors' and society's expectations, it is necessary to know the stories. Because the majority of the stories are unfamiliar today, they are occasionally summarized here. In order to avoid repeated citations of *Aunt Jo's Scrap-Bag*, a system of in-text documentation is used. This system includes volume and page numbers in parentheses following each quotation.

2. Logo for *Aunt Jo's Scrap-Bag* from *My Boys, Etc.*, Vol. 1.

Introduction

In early 1872 the first of a six-volume collection of Louisa May Alcott's short stories was published. She was certain the collection would sell, partly because of the great popularity of her novel *Little Women*, the best-selling book of 1868. Her readers wanted more stories about children, and Alcott knew that she had a flair for writing such stories. Before 1868 two of her books aimed at adult audiences, *Moods* and *Hospital Sketches*, had received mixed reviews and only moderate success. Thomas Niles of Roberts Brothers Publishing Company had repeatedly suggested to Louisa that she write a girls' story similar to those for boys signed "Oliver Optic" and written by William Taylor Adams.[1] So Alcott had written *Little Women* and had followed it with two novels using the same successful formula, *An Old-Fashioned Girl* and *Little Men*. *Little Men* further developed the March family saga of *Little Women*. All of these novels were successful; sales were high.

Editor Thomas Niles wanted to capitalize on the fame and selling power of his famous author. And, although the receipts from *Little Women*, *An Old-Fashioned Girl*, and *Little Men* had enabled Alcott to pay off family debts, to begin to establish the family's financial security, and to pay for a trip to Europe for herself and her sister May, she wanted to provide even more financial security by selling a collection of her short stories.

The notion of collecting stories of successful authors as a money-making scheme was not a new practice in the publishing

of children's literature. One of the most successful and prolific
nineteenth-century children's writers was Samuel B. Goodrich,
author of the Peter Parley books and a businessman who recognized the market and realized the potential for improvement in
children's books. Capitalizing on that market, he wrote his first
Peter Parley book in 1827, *Peter Parley's Tales of America*, and
by 1856 he had written 170 volumes which had sold approxi-
mately seven million copies, about 300,000 annually.[2]

Preparing the collection of short stories would not be time-
consuming for Alcott, as it would be primarily a reprinting of
stories that had originally been published in children's journals
such as *Merry's Museum* and *Youth's Companion*. Alcott decided to collect her stories under the title *Aunt Jo's Scrap-Bag*,
adding several new stories to each volume to provide interest
and increase salability. Clearly both Thomas Niles and Alcott
perceived that this venture would result in a multivolume collection, and during the next ten years, Roberts Brothers published six volumes of *Aunt Jo's Scrap-Bag*.

This study explores the sixty stories that are collected in
the *Scrap-Bag* volumes. I concentrate here on five of the six
volumes—those that contain short pieces written for children.
Shawl-Straps, published in 1872 as Volume Two of *Aunt Jo's
Scrap-Bag*, is a travelogue that recounts Louisa's trip to Europe
with her sister and a friend in 1871. Although the account can
be readily understood and enjoyed by older children, it is also
clearly directed to adults; I am excluding it from major con-
sideration here because of its different genre, subject matter,
and audience.

The five volumes of *Aunt Jo's Scrap-Bag* are each about 200
pages long. The stories for the most part are quite brief because
the editors of the periodicals in which Alcott originally published them limited their length; *Youth's Companion*, for instance, where Alcott published sixteen of the *Scrap-Bag* stories,
limited authors to three-thousand-word stories.[3] When Alcott's
stories exceeded this limitation, they were published in two
parts. Appendix I lists the stories in each volume and the periodicals in which they originally appeared.

One can speculate about the motivations for the curious
choice of *Aunt Jo's Scrap-Bag* as the title for this collection.

Typical of the contradictions that often appear in Alcott's work, the choice is at once an act of self-assurance and deference. It is an act of self-assurance because Alcott (and Niles) were confident enough of her place as a major author of juvenile fiction that they were certain that short, irregular, odd-shaped "scraps" of her writing would sell. As a best-selling author she could call her stories, some of which were carefully crafted, "scraps" without fear of critical ridicule. But there is a suggestion of apology too; Alcott surely knew they were not among her major works. In many cases, they were written hurriedly to meet publication deadlines or to get quick cash to meet an imminent family financial crisis.

A posture of deference in regard to their work was typical of many nineteenth-century female writers. They saw themselves as writing not primarily as artists but as professionals fulfilling a responsibility. A recent study of nineteenth-century female writers portrays them as "professional writers with work to do and a living to be made from satisfactory fulfillment of an obligation to their audience."[4] They wanted to entertain, but they also had a didactic intention—they wanted their readers to learn something in their reading that they could apply to their lives. They combined these goals well, making female readers identify with the heroine's struggle over adversity.[5] Alcott clearly follows the tradition of combining entertainment and didactic intention. This tradition coincided neatly with the goals of the editors who published Alcott's stories and who wanted stories that taught appropriate moral lessons to their readers.

Alcott's presentation of herself as "Aunt Jo" suggests her resignation to the role of maiden aunt. Several of her biographers state that she knew she was married to her writing and that her stories were her children. In comparing herself to her sister Anna, Louisa writes in her journal, "I sell *my* children and though they feed me, they don't love me as hers do."[6] During her year abroad in 1871, her brother-in-law John Pratt had died, causing Louisa's role as aunt and as guardian and provider to her sister Anna's sons to loom larger and more important than it had before that time. In fact, *Little Men*, written while she was abroad and after she heard of John's death, is dedicated to her nephews: "To Freddy and Johnny, the little men to whom she owes some of the best and happiest hours of her life, this book is gratefully dedicated by their loving 'Aunt Weedy.'"

The choice of children as subjects for her fiction continues a tradition of American female authors who had written children's stories, often early in their careers. The tradition goes back at least to the early nineteenth century and the popular author who was a good friend of Louisa's mother, Lydia Marie Child. Although Child was later remembered as an essayist and advice-giver, she also wrote children's stories. Remarkable for its antislavery views, her *Evenings in New England: Intended for Juvenile Amusement and Instruction* (1824) is a collection of essays, tales, and dialogues in which Lucy and Robert question their aunt about history, science, and literature.

Other female authors developed the tradition. Catherine Sedgwick, best known for *A New England Tale* and *Redwood*, also wrote moral tales and juvenile fiction. Eliza Follen wrote several collections of children's stories—*The Well-Spent Hour* and *A Sequel to the Well-Spent Hour*—and edited a juvenile magazine, *Child's Friend*, from 1843 to 1850.[7]

Other female authors wrote stories narrated by maiden aunts. Maria J. McIntosh began her career as a writer of juvenile tales that she published pseudonymously in 1842 and 1843 as "Aunt Kitty's Tales." Narrated by a kindly maiden aunt, the stories are defined by their moralistic subtitles: "Blind Alice, A Tale for Good Children"; "Ellen Leslie, or the Reward of Self-Control"; "Florence Arnott, or Is She Generous"; "Jessie Graham, or Friends Dear but Truth Dearer"; and "Emily Herbert, or The Happy Home."[8] McIntosh also wrote a volume of short stories for adults, *Evenings at Donaldson Manor; or The Christmas Guest* in which the maiden aunt figured as narrator. Like her "Aunt Kitty's Tales," these stories narrated by Aunt Nancy "render amusement subservient to instruction." McIntosh tells us in her preface that their purpose is to teach the "brave and true and faithful heart that 'all things are possible' —that he who clings to the good and the holy amidst temptation and trial, will find peace and light within him, though all without be storm and darkness; and that in a right understanding of and performance of duty . . . lie our true glory and happiness."

In 1846 Caroline Lee Hentz, who later wrote several controversial novels defending slavery, began her career with a collection of previously published children's stories called *Aunt Patty's Scrap Bag*. Aunt Patty, whom "Scherezade herself could not excell in the number and variety of her domestic histories," tells the story of the Worth family children as they cope with various crises of growing up, including the death of their father. Hentz makes it clear that Aunt Patty's role as storyteller is important in shaping the characters of the Worth children when she asks, "Ought any thing to be regarded as insignificant or ridiculous, that draws the mind from the narrow limits of self, opens the avenues of human sympathy, and adds to the sum of human happiness? Is not Aunt Patty . . . thus distilling the honey of life from its waste flowers and weeds, an object worthy of admiration and respect?"

When authors chose to publish their stories under a pseudonym, they often signed themselves "Aunt." Stories on the subject of drinking, *The Temperance Boys* (1858) and *The Brandy Drops* (1858), were pseudonymously signed "Aunt Julia."[9] *Bound Out* by "Aunt Friendly," which enjoyed popularity in 1858, is the story of an orphan who is sent at age ten to work for a farm family.[10]

To summarize, there was a tradition of female writers who wrote children's fiction; many of their stories assumed the narrative posture of a warm, loving, and intelligent maiden aunt. Alcott must have assumed her volumes, however many there might be, would continue that popular tradition. But probably Niles and Alcott were also influenced in their choice of a title by the predominant imagery of patchwork in the concluding story of the first *Scrap-Bag*. Patchwork was part of the feminine art of needlework in which women took odd-shaped, irregular, and miscellaneous pieces of fabric and sewed them together to produce beautiful, useful quilts. Because of the interest created in the varieties and irregular shapes of the fabric, patchwork was thought to be an enjoyable method of teaching the art of needlework to children.

"Patty's Patchwork," one of the finest stories in the Alcott collections, tells of little girl's efforts to make a patchwork quilt, or comforter, for her baby sister from scrap material that her Aunt Pen gives her. Aunt Pen insists that Patty continue to work at the quilt after her baby sister dies, explaining that as Patty puts together the pieces of the quilt the meaning of her life will fall into place. As the patchwork comforts Patty, the stories in the *Scrap-Bags* will comfort their readers. In her biography of Alcott, Madeleine Stern suggests that patchwork is a dominant metaphor for the collection when she describes the planning of the series:

> Together they [Niles and Alcott] discussed the collection for which the young folks were already wildly clamoring. *Aunt Jo's Scrap-Bag* would include several reprints as well as three new tales. Miss Ledyard of Brooklyn would illustrate the book, in which so much interest had already been aroused. It was simple and profitable also to issue such a collection of old and new. All lives were patchwork, and *Aunt Jo's Scrap-Bag* would bring the dark and bright together in harmony.[11]

The first collection, *My Boys*, appeared early in 1872. Alcott hoped it would sell as a holiday item and described it as a Christmas gift "to amuse the large family that has so rapidly and beautifully grown up about me." She wrote in the preface, "I hope that when they promenade in night-caps and gowns to rifle the plump stockings, the little 'dears' will utter an 'oh!' of pleasure, and give a prance of satisfaction, as they pull out this small gift from Aunt Jo's scrap bag." In writing these stories for her nephews as Christmas presents, Alcott was following a family custom—composing poems, stories, or plays as gifts for special occasions was a common practice in the Alcott household. *My Boys* contained fourteen stories: three were written for the volume; eleven were originally published in either *Merry's Museum* or *Youth's Companion*, popular children's periodicals of the day.

Volume three of *Aunt Jo's Scrap-Bag*, subtitled *Cupid and Chow-Chow, Etc.* and published in 1874, comprised ten stories;

two were written for the volume, and eight had been previously published in various children's periodicals. Several had already been reprinted before being collected in this volume. A *Godey's Lady's Book* reviewer praises the stories, which "are written in that peculiar vein which interests alike children and those of older growth." She continues, "For the little ones, there is plenty of incident and adventure, for the elders, a thoughtful portraiture of characters; and a verisimilitude that appeals to both —'Nelly's Hospital' and 'Cupid and Chow-Chow' are each a finished story, and impress themselves upon the childish memory."[12]

The fourth volume, published in 1878 and subtitled *My Girls, Etc.*, included twelve stories, ten of which had been previously published in children's periodicals; six of those ten had already been reprinted before being collected in *My Girls*. A *St. Nicholas* reviewer praises the tales because they "are full of freshness, humor, and wholesome thought, with inimitable touches of playful fancy and tenderness such as have established Miss Alcott's loving rule over the hearts of her readers."[13]

Jimmy's Cruise in the Pinafore, Etc., volume five, appeared in 1879 and contained thirteen stories; six were written for the *Scrap-Bag* and seven had been previously published in *St. Nicholas* and *Youth's Companion*. *Godey's Lady's Book* gave favorable notice to *Jimmy's Cruise*, as it had the previous volumes of the *Scrap-Bag:* "A collection of short stories for children in the genial, chatty, witty vein peculiar to Miss Alcott's writings. They are sure to please those for whom they are written, the boys and girls of the present day."[14]

The volume that was to become the final one, *An Old-Fashioned Thanksgiving, Etc.*, appeared in 1882, when Alcott was fifty years old and suffering ill health, as she did during much of her later life. Only one new story was written for the collection. Two of the stories had appeared in children's periodicals, and eight had been published in 1868 in Alcott's earlier collection of short stories, *Morning-Glories and Other Stories*. Plagued by ill health and numerous family responsibilities, Alcott was forced to recycle old material rather than to create new.

Although Alcott wrote many more than the sixty stories discussed here, we can conclude that Alcott and her editor

Thomas Niles chose what they thought to be her best work; they wanted the series to be successful and profitable. Since only fourteen of the stories were written for the *Scrap-Bags* and since they are similar in every way to the other stories, it is appropriate to treat the entire body of the stories as the great majority of them were originally presented—as publications for children's periodicals.

The first of the *Scrap-Bag* stories to be published was "Nelly's Hospital" (*Our Young Folks*, 1865); the last was "An Old-Fashioned Thanksgiving" (*St. Nicholas*, 1881). The original publication of the stories does not necessarily follow the order of collection in the *Scrap-Bags;* "Nelly's Hospital," for instance, was included in the third volume of the *Scrap-Bag*, published in 1874. The eight stories from *Morning-Glories* that appear in the final volume of the *Scrap-Bag* in 1882 were written fairly early in Alcott's career. Roughly one-third of the previously published *Scrap-Bag* stories had been written before the great success of *Little Women*; two-thirds were written afterward.

The *Scrap-Bag* stories originally appeared in eight children's periodicals: *Youth's Companion* and *Merry's Museum* published nearly half of the stories; *Hearth and Home, The Christian Register*, and *St. Nicholas* published a group; *Harper's Young People, Our Young Folks*, and *Young Folks Journal* published one story each.

The critics who review and discuss the series refer to it as a collection of stories, but they are using the term loosely. Although the majority are stories, the sixty pieces include descriptions, autobiographical sketches and reminiscences, narratives, travelogues, and fables. This combination allows interesting personal and autobiographical insights.

Even though the "stories" were written over a span of nearly twenty years, they are remarkably similar in subject, theme, characterization, style, and tone. The consistency suggests that Alcott understood the conventions within which she was working and that once she found a workable formula she never departed from it. She developed the formula in her early stories and came to understand it even more fully through her year's editorship of *Merry's Museum*, for which she was paid $500 and which began in January 1868.

In fact, 1868, her thirty-sixth year, is a watershed year for
Alcott. During that year she served as editor for *Merry's Museum* and published *Morning-Glories, Little Women,* and twenty-
one short stories, poems, and essays (six of those stories were
eventually reprinted in the *Scrap-Bags*). Never again would she
sustain such a vigorous period of creativity; never again would
she experiment and explore as she had previously. Before those
years her literary alter ego was the vigorous Jo March; afterward
it was the sedate Aunt Jo. Before 1868 there were numerous
rejections and a few acceptances at ten dollars a story; afterward, there were no rejections and Alcott could command the
top market price for her stories. Alcott certainly took pride in
the fact that she was paid well for her writing. It is interesting
that, although she destroyed all the personal entries in her journals, she left intact information about the dates and acceptances
of her stories and the amount she was paid for them.

Her stories pleased the editors of the children's periodicals which published them. As R. Gordon Kelly demonstrates
in his study of children's periodicals from 1865 to 1890, their
editors, who were associated with a functional elite in American society, considered themselves "custodians of morals and
culture" and looked for stories that would be appropriate to
the "peculiar situations and duties of youth."[15] An early prospectus for *Youth's Companion*, in which Alcott was later to
publish many of her stories, declared, "Our children are born
to higher destinies than their fathers. . . . Let their minds be
formed, their heats prepared, and their characters moulded
for the scenes and duties of a brighter day."[16] Indeed, the conservative nature of the magazines continued until the end of
the century and can be explained in part by the fact that the
most popular of the children's magazines were published by
large book-publishing companies. Most of the editors looked
for "well-devised plots" that showed characters engaged in
"healthy thinking" and "brave action." Because Louisa May
Alcott's stories so clearly formed minds, prepared hearts, and
molded characters, these editors were overjoyed to have her
among their contributors.

It is the purpose of this study to show how the sixty stories
in the five volumes of the *Scrap-Bag* fulfill and complement

the goals of the editors of these children's periodicals. The characterizations and conflicts in her stories are defined by a moral code that she makes explicit in two of her stories, and that is the subject of chapter 2. While the code may have developed in part from a set of transcendentalist principles that differed slightly from those of the editors, the basic tenets of the code—labor, love, and hope—fulfilled the moral requirements the editors set.[17]

This study will show how Alcott's stories reflect the cultural traditions of domesticity that made up the world of mid-nineteenth-century children and women. The chapters on children and women describe the roles and expectations that Alcott prescribed for them. They also explain how women's roles grew out of the conventions of domesticity and how the rules women used to guide their teaching are consistent with the child-rearing literature of the nineteenth century. Alcott truly believed both children and young women were meant to fulfill a higher destiny than the previous generation had; her stories showed us examples of children and women who, in her terms, "lead the way."

Many of the periodicals in which Alcott published her stories grew out of the educational needs of the Sunday schools. Her stories were written in the tradition of early Sunday school literature and were intended both to teach and to entertain. Some of the original periodicals were aimed at the entire family, parents as well as children. While the stories cannot tell us, of course, what parents actually did while raising their children, they can provide valuable insights into what they thought was important and the values they held.

Nineteenth-century literature for children is especially enlightening because we have so much information about child-rearing practices of the time. We know that parents wanted to teach their children and that they regarded the teaching story as a powerful tool to assist them in their efforts. As participants in the Calvinistic tradition, they had studied the parables and understood their didactic value. Some of them had studied allegorical stories as children, such as John Bunyan's *Pilgrim's Progress*, a work which Alcott obviously admired and which she drew on in writing *Little Women*. Some of the first books introduced in the colonies were children's books, read to the children by the adults who wanted to teach them religious lessons.

Alcott brings to the tradition of the children's story several gifts: a strong narrative voice and the use of imaginative insights that grow out of her sense of an essential underlying spirit—certainly a transcendental touch inherited from her father and his friends—which imparts a kind of power or magic to what she says. In the chapters that follow, the *Scrap-Bag* stories are examined for what they can tell us about the ascribed characteristics of children's minds and about how parents hoped to shape their children's behavior. The stories are treated primarily as cultural documents and secondarily as works of art. This is an appropriate procedure because Alcott intended that they be interpreted as teaching stories. As did other female writers of the nineteenth century, Alcott wanted her readers to take away a lesson that would help them in their lives.

NOTES

1. Madeleine B. Stern, *Louisa May Alcott* (Norman: University of Oklahoma Press, 1950), p. 173.
2. Anne Scott MacLeod, *A Moral Tale* (Hamden, Conn.: Archon Books, 1975), p. 37.
3. R. Gordon Kelly, *Mother Was A Lady* (Westport, Conn.: Greenwood Press, 1974), p. 39.
4. Nina Baym, *Woman's Fiction* (Ithaca, New York: Cornell University Press, 1978), p. 16.
5. Ibid., p. 17.
6. Ednah D. Cheney, ed., *Louisa May Alcott* (Boston: Roberts Brothers, 1890), p. 195.
7. Baym, *Woman's Fiction*, p. 74.
8. Ibid., p. 87.
9. MacLeod, *A Moral Tale*, pp. 103-104, 109-110.
10. Ibid., p. 47.
11. Stern, *Louisa May Alcott*, p. 224.
12. Anonymous reviewer quoted in Judith C. Ullom, comp., *Louisa May Alcott* (Washington, D.C.: Library of Congress, 1969), p. 57.
13. Ibid., p. 58.
14. Ibid., p. 59.

15. Kelly, *Mother Was A Lady*, pp. 11, 31.

16. Prospectus to *Youth's Companion*, quoted in Lovell Thompson, ed., *Youth's Companion* (Boston: Houghton Mifflin, 1954), p. 2.

17. In treating the stories as publications in children's periodicals and showing how they are consistent with the goals of their publishers, I am following the methodological lead of Richard F. Sykes and R. Gordon Kelly, who believe that it is useful to study literary texts as social and historical documents. In *American Studies: Essays on Theory and Method* (Columbus, Ohio: C. E. Merrill Pub. Co., 1968) Sykes argues that the written artifacts of a culture can be usefully studied to gain an understanding of what people believe about their world. Authors select experiences for their stories that "stimulate certain associations, meanings, prejudices, often of a very ambiguous kind, in the mind of the reader." The way the author shapes characters and their experiences can "tell us something about the expectations of authors and readers, which in turn lead the student to the value patterns of a culture" (p. 90).

Developing the argument of Sykes, R. Gordon Kelly suggests in "Literature and the Historian" (*American Quarterly*, 26 [May 1974], 141-159) that it is helpful to begin with a concept of culture that Clifford Geertz calls "the set of control mechanisms—plans, recipes, rules, instructions—for the governing of behavior." This concept provides a framework within which to examine systematically the social function of literature within various groups of American society. Kelly reasons that "the selective preservation of literary texts" constitutes a kind of human behavior, and he suggests that it is appropriate to study "the rules and definitions which order and govern the creation and consumption of literature" (p. 147).

According to Kelly, nineteenth-century children's books and stories contributed, in part, to the process of children's socialization. While it is difficult to comprehend the meaning of these books for the audience, it is easier to specify the meaning for the author, whose work constitutes a response to his or her cultural milieu. Kelly says that children's literature suggests "the ways in which a group defines and symbolizes the principles of order thought to structure and sustain a given way of life. Children's stories may also define, often quite directly, the limits of permissible behavior in certain circumstances and suggest typical and acceptable modes of reward and punishment." They can also tell us about the strategies of "reassurance and persuasion" employed by the group. And they give us insights into "the group's assumptions about the nature of the reading experience, about the imputed characteristics of children's minds, and about the ways in which changes in personality, belief or styles of behavior may be effected" (Kelly, pp. 154-155). In short, one can examine children's literature to understand a body of knowledge that a group considers essential to its continued existence.

THE PROMISE
OF DESTINY

1

Traditions

The prominence of the moral tale in America, of which Louisa May Alcott's short stories for children are most sophisticated and nearly the last example, grows out of the major status that has been accorded to children in America. From the beginning, children were gifts from God to be treasured, nurtured, and educated in such a way as to provide evidence of the family's good conduct and hope for salvation. Because of this perception, parents paid a great deal of attention to the fate of their children's souls and devoted their energies to ensuring that they were reared and educated in such a way as to attain salvation. Although good habits did not guarantee salvation, they were a channel through which grace could flow.[1] In order to develop good habits in their children, pious parents faced two responsibilities—to instruct and to discipline them. Instruction began at home and later continued in the churches and schools. As early as 1642 Massachusetts passed a law requiring that parents teach their children to read in order that their religious welfare not be overlooked.[2]

The relatively small population and high infant mortality also placed a high valuation on children. The practice of partible inheritance and the ready availability of land created relatively equal opportunity for all children and made it possible for them to be independent at an early age. And the political situation suggested that each child would be important as a future citizen. For these reasons, it was important for parents to educate their children properly, as well as to provide food, shelter, and protection for them.

Children were beginning to play a more prominent role in other countries as well as in America. During the eighteenth century, children had begun to take a more central place in the family, as Philippe Ariès' study of family life in continental Europe has shown.[3] Before that time the family had been characterized by a rather loose structure, and parents had displayed a relative indifference to children, with parents and children sharing few pursuits. There had been an absence of any clear distinction between behavior appropriate for children and adults. But eventually parents became more concerned about matters of children's hygiene, physical health, and education.

Part of this change in the social attitude toward children that began to develop in the eighteenth century can be attributed to John Locke and his influential book, *Some Thoughts Concerning Education*, published in 1690. Locke, who believed the child's mind at birth represented a tabula rasa, a blank sheet, argued for a broader curriculum that included self-discipline for children, opposition to corporal punishment, and a more modern attitude toward childrearing. Eventually, the child's position of utter subordination began to change. After Locke, the education of the child became increasingly social rather than religious in order to prepare the child for gainful employment.

This gentler and more sensitive attitude is part of a wider change in eighteenth-century social attitudes. According to A. J. Plumb, it is "a part of that belief that nature was inherently good, not evil, and what evil there was derived from man and his institutions; an attitude which was also reflected among a growing elite in a greater sensitivity towards women, slaves and animals."[4]

In America, as in England, this increased concern for children can be seen in the way children were educated and reared. The Puritans were, of course, concerned for their children's salvation. By the beginning of the nineteenth century, the notion of infant depravity was still widely held. By 1800 there was still a widespread belief that "the infant child was already intrinsically limited by a heritage of sin and that sin expressed itself most vividly in excess or pride of will. A playful, energetic, pleasure-loving child would surely be on the road to perdition."[5]

The heritage included Jonathan Edwards' words that unrepentant children were "young vipers and infinitely more hateful than vipers." Parents were reminded in sermons that their children were not "too little to die or go to hell."[6]

This approach to childrearing has been identified and described very recently by Philip Greven in *The Protestant Temperament* as one of three he found prevalent in his study of early America. This attitude characterized "evangelicals," who called for a suppression of the self and found it necessary to break the will of the child. In contrast to the evangelicals, and more consistent with the philosophy of childrearing that Alcott adopts in her stories, the "moderates" attempted to bend the will of the child by developing a sense of self-control and by emphasizing the necessity of love and duty. And finally, in the "genteel" families, relationships between parents and children emphasized self-assertion and were characterized by fond affection rather than conscientious discipline.

Whatever a family's childrearing approach might be, children were of central importance. It was primarily the woman's responsibility to take care of the home and to educate her children. If the woman was subservient to her husband in other ways, she at least had a joint "interest in governing the rest of their family."[7] In relation to her children and servants, she had a position of authority equal to her husband, and she played an important role in rearing and educating her children.

By the beginning of the nineteenth century, the work responsibilities of women had changed so that, although they still worked primarily at home, their major responsibilities were for household upkeep and child care. Whereas previously their work had been agricultural and household-based, the development of functional specialization and division of labor changed the nature of women's work. Increasingly, there developed a separation between the work of the home and the rest of the world. It was this convention that defined the nature of domesticity and women's role within that sphere. Although changed in nature, women's major tasks were still rooted in religious motives and rhetoric, as they had been in the seventeenth and eighteenth centuries. Mothers were expected to be pious, setting examples in their own behavior of what they wanted their children to become. The influence of Locke notwithstanding, religious and moral instruction was still important.

CHILDREARING LITERATURE

Nineteenth-century women were assisted in understanding their domestic responsibilities by a host of sermons, essays, stories, and manuals written primarily by New Englanders, who gave advice of all kinds. Many of the authors were women; several knew the Alcott family well. In fact, one of the most popular, the physician William A. Alcott, who wrote *The Young Mother, The Young Wife, A Word to Teachers*, and *The Laws of Health*, was Louisa May Alcott's uncle.

The works of these advice-givers can be divided into five major categories: those dealing primarily with the mother's (occasionally the father's) responsibilities; those offering principles for childrearing; those assessing women's social roles; those discussing education for women; and those devoted to matters of etiquette that prescribed appropriate manners for men and women.[8] Although the works of advice in all categories relate directly to this study of Alcott, the first two are critically important in understanding the pervasive emphasis on children, the responsibility that mothers had for their development, and the way Alcott used related attitudes in her writing.

The authors of these works, which were published mostly in the 1820s, 1830s, and 1840s and found a ready distribution due to a general growth in publishing at that time, were generalists—ministers, homemakers, and teachers—who wrote out of a desire to prepare children for their social and family responsibilities.[9] They may have filled the need for information created by changes in the nature of the family, or they may simply have been preferred over the traditional family sources of advice, which may have been perceived as less trustworthy in an era of great and rapid change.[10] In spite of the fact that the advice manuals cannot tell us what was actually done, they can give us insights about important issues and attitudes relating to children.

The need for these manuals grew out of the change in childrearing approaches from physical coercion to gentle manipulation. Rather than imposing external controls, parents were encouraged to help their children develop internal controls.[11] If the child's internal controls were to be developed and fostered, the next question was how to go about it. Childrearing literature directly addressed this question.

The themes that are commonly developed in the childrearing manuals are, interestingly, the same ones that Bronson Alcott, Louisa's father, adopted in his writing and teaching and, even more to the point here, the ones that prevail in Louisa's short stories. That this is the case should not be surprising, since, as has been mentioned above, the Alcotts knew several of the advice-givers well and, as friends, they discussed childrearing practices and shared common beliefs. Although Bronson never published any works that fall in the category of childrearing literature, his entire life was devoted to understanding and helping children. A comparison of themes in the childrearing literature and Louisa May Alcott's moral tales shows that the moral tale is really the children's counterpart of the adult childrearing literature. The audience and therefore the subject and style change, but the themes are consistent.

Let us examine the major themes of the childrearing literature and briefly explore how Alcott uses them in her stories.[12] First of all, the childrearing literature reveals a new belief in the importance of the child that accompanies both respect for the child and realization that the events and habits of early youth are exceedingly important. Visitors to America such as Alexis de Tocqueville and Harriet Martineau noticed the prominence of the child; several visitors commented on children's irascible behavior and tended to agree that parents treated children as equals. In his analysis of the influence of democracy on the American family, de Tocqueville says that "a species of equality prevails around the domestic hearth." He continues:

> I think that, in proportion as manners and laws become more democratic, the relation of father and son becomes more intimate and more affectionate; rules and authority are less talked of, confidence and tenderness are often-

times increased, and it would seem that the natural bond
is drawn closer in proportion as the social bond is loos-
ened.[13]

As the child was assuming a position of more prominence
in the family, the belief in the notion of infant depravity was
slowly giving way to the notion of infant potential. One of the
first in America to recognize that potential and to dispute the
notion of depravity, as is discussed in more detail in chapter
3, was Bronson Alcott, who might appropriately be thought of
as a great ally of both children and the authors of the books of
advice on how to rear them. This notion of infant potential
was fundamental to both romantic and transcendental thought,
and it shows itself as fundamental in Louisa May Alcott's writing through her choice of the study and development of children as her major subject. The few obvious exceptions are several books written before the success of *Little Women*—*Moods*,
Hospital Sketches, and her gothic thrillers written under the
pen name of A. M. Barnard.

Closely related to the central importance of childhood in
the childrearing literature is a second notion that childhood offered the best opportunity for parents to shape their children's
behavior. The Puritan tradition and the American practices that
grew out of it in the eighteenth century had taken this adult
responsibility very seriously. So did the essays and manuals of
the early nineteenth century, and they promised heartening rewards. Louisa's father, who devoted his life to the rearing of
his children and to improving education for children, saw the
task as an opportunity to perfect humankind. The formulas
spelled out in the childrearing literature were engaging, and
their promise of success carried over to Louisa May Alcott's
short fiction. The parents who teach and the children who overcome, whatever their conflict may be, succeed. For the most
part, these are and-they-all-lived-happily-ever-after stories; but
the naiveté and innocent wonder suggested by that cliché is
countered by the great effort the children put forth and the
moral responsibility they accept to bring about success.

Thirdly, the childrearing essayists assumed that parents, most
especially mothers, played a critical role in the rearing of children. The actual work and responsibility of the mother in rela-

tionship to the child had probably changed very little over the years: the mother had always taken care of the very young. It was, rather, the awarding of significance to the mother's role and its social perception that had changed.[14] This emergence of the women's sphere gave, as we have seen, new prominence and responsibility to women.

If the child is at the center of Alcott's works, women are their most important adjuncts. The children are protagonists, but they are portrayed in settings of the home where the mother is central. Mothers in Alcott's fiction advise and set examples. They are gentle, reasonable humans who respond warmly and emotionally to children's needs. Most important, they acknowledge their children; they assign importance to their feelings and emotional needs. In short, they are fictional portrayals of what the advice-givers would have described as ideal mothers. Even in Alcott's gothic thrillers, where women are ruthless and conniving, mothers still show love and a sense of devotion to their children.

A fourth important point is that authors of childrearing literature gave major responsibility for childrearing tasks to women rather than men. Although men were occasionally chastized for ignoring their children, it was conceded that they did not play a major role in childrearing, at least not until the children were much older.

Men in Alcott's short stories play a minor role. They are two-dimensional characters at the fringes of the drama who take little part in it. They are not evil, nor do they oppose the beliefs and actions of the women. The women, in fact, assume they have the support of the men around them. It is easy to think of Alcott's short fiction without adult males entirely; the only major male characters are young, as those in *Little Men* and *Jo's Boys*.

Why males play such a minor role in Alcott's fiction is an intriguing question for students of Alcott's fiction. The most obvious reason is that Alcott is describing realistic domestic dramas, and fathers who leave the home to earn a living for their families forego any important role in the domestic drama. The women are strong and forthright with such a sense of solidarity that they need no men to give credence to their actions. The curious question that arises in the case of Alcott's fiction is why

this is the case when her own father played such a critical role
in her childhood. Partly because Alcott destroyed all personal
materials in her journals, we can only speculate. Perhaps she
perceived her father's role as too overbearing, perhaps she perceived him as a failure, or perhaps this curious omission is
simply an indication that, for Alcott, the mother was more
critical. This is more a matter for Alcott's biographers to settle.
Whatever the motivation, the net result is that Alcott's women
succeed in getting things done. The same elevation in the status
of women that appears in the childrearing literature also appears
in Alcott's fiction.

A fifth theme in the childrearing literature argues for the interconnectedness of spirit, mind, and body. The authors believed that there was a direct relationship between the child's
physical condition, mental health, and moral character. Both
of Catharine Beecher's popular books, *The American Women's
Home* and *Treatise on Domestic Economy*, explained the importance of this connection. Every scholar who has studied
nineteenth-century childrearing acknowledges the importance
of this concept. For example, Bernard Wishy shows how these
writers emphasized the connection between daily "laws of
health" and moral strategy,[15] and Anne L. Kuhn points out
how these concerns of food for body and spirit elevated the
humble role of the housewife to a new status.[16] The authors
of childrearing literature were very specific about their recom-
mendations for proper health and nutrition: diet should be
simple and nutritious; clothing should have a simplicity and
modesty of design to allow freedom of movement; exercise and
play should encourage creative development and, in so doing,
prevent moral flabbiness and laziness.

Bronson Alcott surprised New Englanders early in the nineteenth century when he adopted these principles in the schools
in which he taught before they were spelled out formally in any
published prose. His schools were comfortable, and the curriculum included plenty of activity. He was personally preoccu-
pied with finding a proper diet, and Louisa and her sisters had
suffered through some of the extreme dietary regimens he prescribed, among them an apples-and-water program that he
adopted while his utopian experiment at Fruitlands was in prog-

ress. Louisa acknowledges the importance of good nutrition and emphasizes in her fiction again and again how it can create a sound mind as well as a sound body.

Finally, as part of the move away from corporal punishment, childrearing literature insisted that parents should teach their children self-control through obedience. Obedience in childhood would lead to self-control in adulthood. It was understood that control would not be taught through coercion, but rather through parental example. In addition to providing an excellent model, parents taught self-control by appealing to the conscience as the central authority over children. Henan Humphrey, author of *Domestic Education*, maintains that a child cannot disobey without self-condemnation once conscience has been established. He says:

> *Command* your child, and if he sees you are in earnest, he will probably obey you. Show him the reason of the command, and he will yield more cheerfully. Appeal to his conscience, and get that enlisted on your side, and you have a hold on him which you never had before. You have gained an auxiliary, that . . . will often be more efficient when you are absent, than when you are present.[17]

Those who wrote on the rearing and teaching of children insisted upon the exercise of conscience to establish self-control. Bronson Alcott, while one of them, was not the first to argue for such a goal. As we have seen, John Locke had called for the use of reason earlier. And the Puritans had been encouraged to use bodily punishment only as a last resort, as Edmund S. Morgan explains: "Ministers who wrote and spoke on the subject almost always counseled their readers and listeners to win children to holiness by kindness rather than to try to force them to it by severity."[18]

Many of the authors of childrearing literature linked the need for self-control to proper moral behavior. Louisa May Alcott takes the development of self-control as the major lesson that the children in her fiction must learn as they grow up, a lesson just as important for boys as it is for girls. Critics have argued that control was the way by which the patriarchal society kept women operating on its terms, but in Alcott's fiction the lessons of control are just as difficult and important for the boys as for the girls.

These important themes in the childrearing literature—the importance of the child, the realization that childhood offered great opportunities for shaping habits and behavior, the elevated and central role of the mother as teacher of children, the interrelationships between mind and body, and the importance of teaching self-control—suggest the values that authors at that time held about children and what they hoped to teach them. These themes also provide the framework for the family in Alcott's fiction.

THE MORAL TALE

Part of this great body of childrearing literature, but by no means all of it, was written by ministers and others affiliated with religous institutions of the day. The Reverend John S. C. Abbott's *The Mother at Home* may have been the first best-seller on domestic education.[19] Timothy Dwight, a pastor-teacher who eventually became president of Yale, wrote *The Father's Book;* and Reverend Horace Bushnell wrote *Views on Christian Nurture*, which combined elements from Calvinist, Enlightenment, and Romantic theories.[20]

Those who were involved in religious organizations also approached the proper rearing of children from another point of view. In addition to writing essays and manuals similar to those mentioned above, which were directed at adult audiences, they also began to write and supervise publication of moral tales directed at children themselves. Many of the publishing activities grew out of the American Sunday School Union, which was founded in 1824 "as part of the great evangelical movement of the early nineteenth century" and which united the Sunday school efforts of the major evangelical Protestant sects.[21] By 1830 this union had issued nearly six million copies of Sunday school works for both children and adults.[22]

Their decision to begin publishing fiction was not taken lightly, for it was commonly thought that fiction could have a dangerous influence on youth. That Alcott was sensitive to the point of view of those who regarded fiction dubiously is readily apparent in "Fancy's Friend" (VI, 208-234), the concluding story of the final *Scrap-Bag* volume.[23] The story has the tone of a fable and is obviously meant to teach a moral lesson, but the characters—Fact, Fiction, and Fancy—are human. Alcott uses allegory here to suggest the distrust of fantasy-like tales that many adults felt at that time. She concedes that their point is well taken, although she does so reluctantly and with a sense of great loss.

Fancy is a young girl who is visiting the seashore with her Uncle Fact and Aunt Fiction. Aunt Fiction is "a graceful picturesque woman; who told stories charmingly, wrote poetry and novels, was very much beloved by young folks, and was the friend of some of the most famous people in the world" (218). Uncle Fact is a direct contrast to Aunt Fiction; he is

> a grim, grave, decided man; whom it was impossible to bend or change. He was very useful to every one; knew an immense deal; and was always taking notes of things he saw and heard, to be put in a great encyclopaedia he was making. He didn't like romance, loved the truth, and wanted to get to the bottom of every thing. (218)

Fancy's name captures her personality. Although Alcott tells us that "the lessons of both were necessary to her, as to all of us," the story's conflict revolves around whether Fact or Fiction will govern Fancy's life. Interestingly, as the tenor of the times would lead us to suspect, Fact wins, although the impact of Fiction remains in Fancy's life.

The conflict develops when Fancy brings home a friend, Lorelei, who emerged in human form from a fantasy mermaid that Fancy created at the beach. Clearly Lorelei represents the role of fantasy in the life of a child. While Aunt Fiction sees the positive value that Fancy's association with Lorelei can have, Uncle Fact disapproves because Lorelei is a waif who can only sing, dance, and tell stories and cannot read or write. Even

when Lorelei sings a song with "what your uncle calls a moral
to it," Uncle Fact still wants to send Lorelei away, because she
is a "sly, bad child." In a question-answer session that is similar
in format and tone to those Louisa's father had recorded of his
conversations with his daughters in his *Observations* and to the
teaching sessions that Elizabeth Peabody records of Temple
School, Uncle Fact quizzes Fancy about the value of her friend
Lorelei:

> "Didn't Luly [Uncle Fact's name for Lorelei] want
> you to deceive us, and every one else, about who she
> was?"
> "Yes, sir."
> "Don't you like to be with her better than with your
> aunt or myself?"
> "Yes, sir."
> "Hadn't you rather hear her songs and stories than
> learn your lessons?"
> "Yes, sir."
> "Isn't it wrong to deceive people, to love strangers
> more than those who are a father and mother to you,
> and to like silly tales better than useful lessons?"
> "Yes, sir."
> "Very well. Then, don't you see, that, if Luly makes
> you do these wrong and ungrateful things, she is not a
> good child, nor a fit playmate for you?" (231)

Although he recognizes that Fancy is sad, he counsels her to
give up Lorelei, for she will lead only to trouble. Following
Lorelei, she races to the shore, but when she arrives she sees
nothing but "the scattered pebbles, shells, and weeds that
made the mock mermaid, floating away on a receding wave"
(233). Once surrendered, Lorelei reappears only in Fancy's
memory.

"Fancy's Friend" is important in understanding Alcott's
work and the early nineteenth-century attitude toward literature for children. As Fact is married to Fiction, reality is
wedded to the imagination. Although near opposites, they
make a strong team, with one counterbalancing the other. Al-

though Fact is yoked to Fiction in an indissolvable relationship and hence recognizes her validity, Fiction is not an appropriate guide for life. The encyclopedia is more useful and gives
validity to reality in a way that Fiction cannot. A child who
is already prone to succumb to the whims of the imagination,
as Fancy was to Lorelei, is especially susceptible and therefore
in need of the countervailing force of reality to provide balance. Even though the fantasy-friend Lorelei is willing to sing
a song with a moral tale in which a steadfast rock is valued over
a fragile yet headstrong bubble, she ultimately must be yielded,
with a sense of great sadness and loss, to reality.

Another clue to the interpretation of Lorelei's character can
be found in the connection with her namesake. Lorelei introduces herself, saying, "Call me by my German cousin's pretty
name." Her "German cousin" is a fairy in a German legend
similar to the Greek sirens who lived on a rock at river's edge
and whose singing lured sailors to their death. In Heinrich
Heine's ballad "Lorelei," which Alcott is likely to have read,
Lorelei is "a lovely maiden . . . so wondrous fair" who sits at
water's edge on a mountainous rock in which fate and beauty
are united. While Lorelei's melody, "song of mysterious power," floats down from the rocky summit, the base of the cliff
brings catastrophe to the boatman of a small skiff who is overwhelmed with "turbulent love": "No longer he marks where
the cliff is, / He looks to the mountains above."[24] The boatman is distracted by Lorelei's melody, which ultimately be-
trays him. Alcott seems to be suggesting in her moral tale that,
as Lorelei's melody distracts the boatman in Heine's poem, the
"melody" of Fiction distracts the young readers of the moral
tale.

As Alcott's reasoning in "Fancy's Friend" was largely prag-
matic, so was the decision of the Sunday School Union. The
reading public wanted stories by Americans about America.
Lydia Marie Child says in her preface to *Evenings in New En-
gland*—a subtitle informs the reader it is "Intended for Juvenile
Amusement and Instruction"—"Excellent as those books [by
Miss Edgeworth and Mrs. Barbauld] are, they are emphatically
English; and I indulged the hope that American scenes, and
American characters, would give a delightful locality to the fol-

lowing stories." If children were more likely to read stories
than religious tracts and essays, then the Sunday School Union
would furnish such stories, provided they were written " in
strict accordance with truth and nature."[25] There was little distinction between most Sunday school stories and those published by secular publishing companies.[26] The fact that the Sunday School Union saw fiction primarily as an instrument for
moral instruction made little difference. Almost all fiction for
children in the early part of the nineteenth century was justified by its didactic properties. As Child did in *Evenings in New
England*, authors were careful to point out the instructive qualities of their work. Samuel Goodrich writes in his preface to
Parley's Book of Fables, "I am well aware that conscientious
scruples are entertained by many wise and good people as to
the use of fiction in juvenile books, but it appears to me that
the argument commonly lies against the *abuse* and not against
the *use* of fiction."[27] And in one of Child's dialogues between
an aunt and her niece Lucy, called "History," the aunt responds
to Lucy's question about whether it is wicked to read novels
and plays by reasoning, "It is, no doubt, wrong to read such
books very frequently,—and very unprofitable to read them at
all, without much discrimination; but everything is valuable according to its *use*; and when lighter kinds of reading serve to
impress something more valuable on our minds, they answer an
exceedingly good purpose."[28] It was also clear that moral concerns were of greater import than intellectual ones. It was, after
all, moral training that shaped character. As one fictional mother put it, "It is far better that [one] should know how to be
kind and gentle to those around him than to understand all the
poetry, or all the science that was ever written."[29]
    Although the moral tale had great success in America for
reasons that were part of a national impulse and therefore
unique, the flowering of the moral tale was not only an American development. In his discussion of children on the Conti-
nent, Philippe Ariés notes that there came a time near the end
of the sixteenth century when "certain pedagogues refused to
allow children to be given indecent books any longer."[30] This
led eventually to the adoption of expurgated editions of classics
for children. J. H. Plumb has pointed out how the growth in

children's literature in eighteenth-century England was related
to the new interest in and respect for the child. Such entrepre-
neurial publishers as Thomas Boreman and John Newbery
"scented a market for books that would be simple in presentation, enticing to the eye, and written specifically for children."[31] But, of course, since adults were the ones who bought
the books, new children's literature "was aimed at the young,
but only through the refraction of the parental eye."[32]

The man who was quickest to exploit the market in England
was John Newbery, who published a wide range of children's
books covering topics such as geography, history, natural history, and adaptations of the classics. He also produced quanti-
ties of moral tales, probably more beloved by parents, Plumb
suspects, than by children. The moral tales were eventually
followed in England by novels for children—the first in 1783—
and lending libraries for these works appeared around the turn
of the century.[33] These books were being produced more and
more cheaply and soon were in demand by and became available to the industrious working class, particularly "those families where social ambition had been stirred by the growing opportunities of a new industrializing society."[34]

CHILDREN'S PERIODICALS

Publishers of secular children's periodicals in America, who
provided a powerful ally to the American Sunday School
Union, were motivated to meet the needs of the same audience that Newbery and others were meeting in England—the
"industrious middle class." Publishers of these periodicals
had virtually the same goals as publishers of religious materials:
to instill a sense of nationalistic pride and to help shape the
future of the republic and to provide a moral direction for
children. Together these publishers shaped the direction of
children's literature. The writers who contributed to these
publications felt that "the American future held as much responsibility as opportunity . . . as much threat of collapse as
promise of fulfillment."[35] They believed that democracy
would succeed if the moral qualities of its citizens were strong
enough. No task was more important, therefore, than the mor-

al education of the nation's youth. Writers of juvenile literature, of course, could contribute to this task. And that is how
a "juvenile literature, conscientiously designed to 'enlarge the
circle of knowledge, to invigorate the understanding, to
strengthen the moral nerve, to purify and exalt the imagination' came into being, not to entertain children but to prepare
them for their momentous role in the preservation of the Republic."[36]

Periodicals for children helped insure the success of juvenile
literature because they offered a vehicle for circulation of authors' stories. Publication of these periodicals began in the early
nineteenth century. Their publishers and editors hoped that the
periodicals would help children realize the promise of American
life in the same way that the authors of the moral tales and
childrearing advice did. Nathaniel Willis, the founder of *Youth's
Companion*, one of the longest-running of these journals, declared that "our children are born to higher destinies than their
fathers." He exclaimed, "Let their minds be formed, their
hearts prepared, and their characters moulded for the scenes
and duties of a brighter day."[37] He proposed that the *Youth's
Companion* would be

> a small weekly journal, which should entertain . . . chil-
> dren and insensibly instruct them; which should occupy
> leisure hours, and turn them to good account; which
> should sanction and aid parental counsel and pulpit ad-
> monition; which should, in an easy and familiar manner,
> warn against the ways of transgression, error and ruin,
> and allure to those of virtue and piety.[38]

The prospectus to *Youth's Companion*, written in 1827, emphasized its moral purpose, a commitment common to these
early periodicals: "it will aim to inculcate truth by brief narratives, familiar illustrations, short biographies, and amusing an-
ecdotes."[39] It would, in short, emphasize the "truly useful"
and avoid the frivolous or injurious.

Literally hundreds of such periodicals were published during
the nineteenth century. Many ceased publication during the
Civil War, and many were initiated after the war. R. Gordon

Kelly, in a recent study of periodicals published after the war, argues that the majority were edited by conservative men; some of them were owned by conservative book-publishing houses, who wanted to preserve the tradition of gentility and offer genteel values as a solution to the instability and problems that characterized the Gilded Age.[40]

The editors, who were not necessarily wealthy but who had a commitment to culture and discipline, believed in the genteel spirit that honored the virtues of truth, fortitude, prudence, and justice. They had, in Emerson's words, "a wide affinity for the world" and believed, as he did, that the gentleman was "a man of truth, the lord of his own actions, and expressing that lordship in his behavior; not in any manner dependent and servile, either on persons, or opinions, or possessions. Beyond this fact of truth and real force, the word denotes good-nature or benevolence: manhood first, and then gentleness."[41] The editors of the representative periodicals that Kelly studies possessed genteel characteristics and fitted Emerson's definition of a gentleman. Such editors as Daniel Ford, John Townsend Trowbridge, and Daniel Lothrop believed that the ideal social expression could be modeled on a traditional gentleman, and they used their position to shape a gentry code and to present that code to Americans in their magazines.[42]

According to Kelly, the fiction published in five major periodicals—*Our Young Folks* (1865-1872), *Riverside Magazine for Young People* (1867-1870), *St. Nicholas* (1873-1939), *Wide Awake* (1875-1893), and *Youth's Companion* (1827-1929)—embodies genteel notions and values, and is representative of that published in most children's periodicals between 1865 and 1890, the period that has been called the golden day of children's literature. The editors of those journals, along with the authors of etiquette books, believed that society would be better if "all its members were perfect gentlemen and true ladies." He continues, "Those who wrote for and edited the children's periodicals . . . made every effort to delineate that society in their domestic fiction, to dramatize in an entertaining but truthful fashion the necessary and sufficient basis in individual character of personal achievement, social order, and progress in a democratic society."[43]

Kelly's work is important to consider here because Alcott originally published her stories in these same periodicals: *Youth's Companion* originally published sixteen *Scrap-Bag* stories, *St. Nicholas* published six, and *Our Young Folks* published one. In addition, twelve more of the *Scrap-Bag* stories were published in the late 1860s in *Merry's Museum*, which had an editorial policy and audience similar to the others and which, in fact, was absorbed by *Youth's Companion* in the early 1870s. In other words, well over half of the *Scrap-Bag* stories were published in periodicals that can be said to embody the values of the genteel society.

It is interesting that Alcott published several of her gothic thrillers, anonymously, of course, in a periodical quite different from the others—*Frank Leslie's Illustrated Newspaper*. The editorial standards of this weekly contrast sharply with the standards of the others in their use of brutality, violence, and lack of personalization, and Frank Leslie's personal flamboyance differed from the conservative nature of the other editors.[44] The vast difference in the nature of her gothic thrillers and her moral tales serves to validate Kelly's point about the differences in the publications.

A *Scrap-Bag* story that exemplifies very clearly Alcott's alliance with gentry values is "A Curious Call" (I, 111-121). In it, the gentry ideals are symbolized by the golden eagle from the Boston City Hall Dome, which appears before the narrator in a sort of dream and describes how the statues of Boston come to life at night. Not surprisingly, their behavior is consistent with the values of the cultural elite. The eagle makes very clear the code by which he operates when he says to the narrator, "I am a gentleman; therefore I behave myself" (116). The statues, the most prominent of which is one of Benjamin Franklin, are aware of the current issues of the day and work to make life better for all. In fact, the eagle admonishes the narrator to look about her for good things to do and to make them the subject of her stories. He says, "Look about you. People are so wrapped up in their own affairs they don't do half they might" (121). The life of the mind is important, but so is the health of the body. The statues, for example, those of Goethe and Schiller, are hearty and vigorous and admire the beauty in women of "straight shoulders, well-opened chests, and an upright figure, firmly planted on active feet" (119). In short, the story introduces the important themes of gentry fiction into children's periodicals. The eagle, who symbolizes gentry values, suggests behavior that will be effective in maintaining the strength of the country. The gentleman's behavior is highly moral and is apparently instinctive to those who possess good intentions, education, concern for others, and awareness of public issues. Particularly absent from the requirements of the gentleman is wealth. One can become a gentleman, or a lady, merely by acting like one.

In order to describe the fiction and its relationship to the socialization process of children of the Gilded Age, Kelly outlines several narrative formulas that characterize fictional elements of the stories. In doing so, he follows John Cawelti's use of formula as a "conventional system for structuring cultural products." The formula, "a frequently repeated sequence of plot and character elements," can be used as "a common ground on which a relatively small group of producers meets with a particular audience."[45] The use of formula in children's stories helps, in part, to define the socialization process for them. These formulas—the ordeal, the change of heart, and the gentry mission (less important and a variation of the change of heart)—are worth exploring in detail here because they coincide with the formulas in Alcott's fiction.

In the ordeal formula story, a young girl or boy is temporarily removed, for one reason or another, from the moral influence of adults. While without this adult supervision and protection, the child finds himself or herself confronted with an experience that calls for decisive action. Typically the child must act quickly, with little time for thought, often responding through force of instinct. After the child resolves the experience acceptably, he or she returns to the protection of the adult world and is rewarded.[46] Kelly points out that the adults who were writing these stories, such as Alcott, often chose to dramatize the kinds of trials and temptations confronting the isolated child, to whom they were particularly sensitive.[47] Further, he explains that the narrative rhythm suggests the movement of phases of ritual rites of passage—"separation from society, a

period of isolation and transition, and finally incorporation
into a new social world or reintegration with the old."[48]

To illustrate the ordeal formula he uses "Bonfires," an Alcott story published in *Youth's Companion* but not one of
those collected in the *Scrap-Bags*. In "Bonfires" twelve-year-
old Phebe risks a storm and a strange landscape to warn an approaching train of a washed-out bridge. Of course, the passen-
gers, who are ladies and gentlemen, reward and praise Phebe,
whose courage and determination to save the train seem to
have been nurtured through her communion with nature, as
she is separated from adults who might have helped her. Her
father is away, her mother is ill, and the neighbors are too dis-
tant to be of any help.[49] Again and again in the *Scrap-Bag* stories, a child is isolated from his or her family and/or society
and is forced to manage without the usual framework of expectation and relationships.

The *Scrap-Bag* story that represents the ordeal formula most
perfectly is "Little Gulliver" (VI, 163-177). This story, one of
the best in the *Scrap-Bag* collections, combines many good elements of the children's story, not the least of which is an in-
genious combination of the heroic talking animal and a lesson
in race relations. The story takes its title from Gulliver, a pet
seagull that lives on the island home of Dan, a lighthouse keeper, and his nephew Davy. The richly woven plot of the story
incorporates three ordeals—one of the lighthouse keeper, and,
more important, two of the children in the story, Davy and a
little black girl named Moppet. The ordeals develop when Dan
leaves the island for supplies. Very soon a storm arises, causing
Dan's boat to crash and wash ashore on the coast. Gulliver, who
goes for help, is captured by a rich, spoiled white girl, but Moppet, her black servant, sympathizes with Gulliver's captivity and
frees him and helps him recover his strength.

Although living with a white family, Moppet is obviously isolated from the support network the family offers. She says,
"Nobody in de world keres fer me. Dey sold me way from my
mammy when I was a baby, and I'se knocked roun eber since.
De oder chilen has folks to lub an kere fer em, but Moppet's
got no friends" (170). She is obviously compassionate, and
when Gulliver discovers Dan near her home, she nurses him

back to health. In reward for her fine care, Old Dan adopts
Moppet and takes her to his island to live with him and Davy.
In the meantime, Davy's ordeal has been to remain alone and
carry out the lighthouse keeper's duty of lighting the lamp to
guide ships into the harbor. In the end the three characters,
like Phebe in "Bonfires," have been isolated from traditional
support systems, have proven their ability to survive through
stamina and strength of character, and have been reunited in
a warm and loving family circle. The life on the island will be
rich and the three will "never tire of its wonders." The implication is, as it is in "Bonfires," that Davy has grown strong
and intelligent through his communion with nature, a theme
that is prevalent in children's fiction of the time.

In the second formula, the change-of-heart, the author often
proceeds according to the ordeal's pattern of separation, isolation, and incorporation. The difference is that in these stories
the child "proceeds from a moral stance that varies from the
merely inappropriate and embarrassing to one that is personally
dangerous and socially vicious."[50] The key element in the
change-of-heart formula is a moral conversion, "a dramatic shift
in perception, which combines a conscious recognition of the
erroneous nature of the individual's former behavior with a conscious resolution to do better."[51]

Alcott includes a number of change-of-heart stories in the
Scrap-Bag collection. These changes of heart are brought about
in Alcott's stories in several ways, but they all embody the necessary dramatic shift in perception. The shift may be coaxed
along by various helpful adults, sometimes parents, and sometimes adults who are not of the direct family circle and who
therefore bring objectivity and understanding that help the
child to the enlightened attitude.

Alcott's children also come to this change of heart through
their own agency, a variation that is not surprising, give Alcott's perception of the child as infinitely wise. These changes
are often the results of insights that come to the children
through moments of inspiration, through dreams, or through
their consciences. How children learn from these insights and
use them to teach others is the subject of the chapter on the
promise of youth.

The majority of Alcott's *Scrap-Bag* stories are not change-of-heart tales because many of her fictional children began as exceedingly wise, they have little need for improvement. In fact, Alcott incorporates an interesting variation of the change-of-heart formula that constitutes a greater number of stories than either of the first two categories. Rather than having the child change from irresponsible to responsible, Alcott alters the procedure and creates conflicts in which the child teaches adults so that they are the ones who undergo the change of heart. For example, young, poor girls often teach older, richer "social butterflies" the lesson that "all fashion demands is composure and self-content."[52] Helen in "Red Tulips" (IV, 205-217) learns through Betty, a young, poor black girl that "she was something better than a butterfly." And Belle in "Roses and Forget-Me-Nots" (IV, 64-86) learns from an errand girl named Lizzie not to be lazy and to be sensitive to the needs of the poor.

Perhaps it was Alcott's recognition of the notion that there is little suspense in the change-of-heart stories because there is little possibility for moral failure that led her to realize the dramatic appeal of a child engaging an adult in some sort of change of heart. Alcott's reversal of the change-of-heart formula is similar to the less important third formula whose basis is "a figure who embodies the moral values of gentility and whose moral force brings about a change in the values of others."[53]

Understanding the narrative formulas and Alcott's variation on them is helpful because the formulas illustrate the similarity between the structure of fictional experience and the socialization process of children. A child is thrust into a world of established patterns of behavior and must learn how to interpret and deal with them through interaction with others. The child learns these elements of the social world through the concept of role, "a pattern of expected behavior associated with a given social status or position in a social structure," which allows the child to communicate and express himself.[54] Children become socialized by learning what is expected of them in the various roles and statuses they assume. Only gradually do they lose the egocentrism that characterizes the very young child and come to possess a sense of self.

Both the ordeal and the change-of-heart formulas dramatize
the origins of self for the child. The young reader perceives the
effectiveness of the values and attitudes that are demonstrated
by the ordeal and the effectiveness of the altered way of acting
in the change-of-heart formula and, to the extent that he or she
participates vicariously in the story, is able to internalize them
and hence solidify his or her sense of self.[55] On the other hand,
the author is presenting through the formulas the values and/or
behavior that she finds acceptable for children in a society that
is rapidly changing. We have already seen in the earlier discussion of common themes in the childrearing-advice literature and
in Alcott's short stories how these values and attitudes are consistent in both genres. The childrearing literature was aimed at
adults, and the Alcott short stories were aimed at children, but
the message in both was similar. The moral tale made the message easier to bear for the reader while it gave the author a vehicle that avoided preaching, as the early leaders of the American Sunday School Union had realized when they decided to
publish moral tales at the beginning of the century.

THE CONVENTIONS OF DOMESTICITY

The focus of our discussion so far has been to understand
the perception of and expectations for children that Alcott
brings to her stories and the conventions of the moral tale and
children's periodicals. But nearly as important as the world of
children is the world of women. In childhood the masculine
and feminine worlds converge but as females mature their
world diverges from that of males. The adult world in Alcott's
stories is a world of women and children. Alcott is portraying
in her fiction the world that Carroll Smith-Rosenberg describes
in her article, "The Female World of Love and Ritual," on relations between women in nineteenth-century America. Central
to this world is "an inner core of kin" consisting of mothers,
daughters, sisters, cousins, aunts, and nieces.[56] These women
play a major role in each other's lives, providing a sense of security, support, and self-esteem. At the heart of this female
world is an intimate mother-daughter relationship. It is through
this relationship that women learned what was expected of them

—Smith-Rosenberg calls it an apprentice system—in preparing to master domestic skills and in seeking a husband. The female rituals that accompany married life, such as pregnancy, childbirth, nursing, weaning, miscarriage, sickness, and death, all involve same-sex activity and hence caused women to have a strong emotional proximity to one another.

That this is so is not surprising because the rigid gender-role definition of the conventions of domesticity led to the emotional segregation of men and women, while the biological realities of frequent pregnancies, childbirth, and menopause bound women together. As a result, a specifically female world built around single-sex networks evolved. Etiquette books, sermons, guides, and private correspondence supported these networks.

This concept of the nineteenth-century women's world provides a proper perspective for understanding the women's world that Alcott describes in her fiction. Her women encompass the many roles that women assume—grandmother, wife, daughter, widow, and spinster. At the center of Alcott's fiction, as of the nineteenth-century woman's world, is the mother-daughter relationship. Even though later chapters describe the influence that Louisa's father had on the themes in her stories, that influence is of secondary importance. At the core of Alcott's most important work, *Little Women*, is the relationship between Marmee and her daughters. It is generally accepted that this novel is highly autobiographical and, in fact, describes the relationship between Abigail Bronson and her four daughters. The novel might be described as a mother's attempt to teach her daughters the female world of love and ritual. Soon after Louisa's birth Bronson wrote of his wife, "Abba will soon be restored to the discharge of those domestic and maternal duties in which she takes so much delight and in the performance of which she furnishes so excellent a model for imitation. . . . She was formed for domestic sentiment rather than the gaze and heartlessness of what is falsely called 'society.' "[57] If, in fact, it is Bronson who suggests the themes to Louisa in real life, it is the mother who teaches them to the children in all her fiction.

Although the mother-daughter relationship is central, aunts also play a major role of support and guidance for their nieces. The important role of maiden aunts is possible because they are less busy than mothers, are often more widely read and traveled, and can use their time and objectivity to solve problems and to understand relationships that are beyond the ken of the immediate family circle. Grandmothers are also present as elders who symbolize the status that the wife and mother achieves after her great work is done. Although the women in the fiction demonstrate negligible power in the lives of men, they possess status and power in the lives of other women.

The behavior of the mothers in Alcott's fiction is characterized by its selflessness. To some extent all of the characters are taught, often through example, to work for the good of others; to do so is part of the gentry ideal, as Alcott suggests in "A Curious Call." But it is the mother in Alcott's fiction who devotes herself to others. Rose in *Rose in Bloom* bemoans her fate, that she has no special gift, that she cannot be "something splendid," such as a great writer, or singer, or poet. Her uncle responds that her gift is "the art of living for others . . . patiently and sweetly."[58] In the *Scrap-Bag* stories, the young women who finally gain insights into the importance of the selfless life and realize the importance of dedicating themselves to others are then worthy of marriage to the ideal suitor who has been waiting for them to come to this realization. This sense of selflessness is especially important for wealthy, young women, who are more likely to be self-indulgent than their poorer counterparts. When they begin to live for others, they begin to take themselves seriously and are thereby qualified to leave what Emily Dickinson calls "that other state" and marry to become "Czar," "Woman," "Wife." Selflessness is one of the important conventions of domesticity that Nancy Cott describes in *The Bonds of Womanhood*. Women were to reject the self-interest of the marketplace and make the home "a sanctuary of 'disinterested' love."[59]

In Alcott's fiction the selflessness is less a burden than it might be because her women marry for love. Any marriage without it would be repugnant to them and therefore out of the question. The fictional Alcott women are very particular about their husbands; having chosen the "perfect" one, they can be assured that he will support their various endeavors. Having taken the marriage vows, husband and wife go their separate ways, he to the marketplace and she to the home, and there is, in fact, little mixing of responsibilities and duties.

Alcott focuses on the moral and intellectual rather than the sexual determinants of the female character. This works itself out in Alcott's fiction as a source of great power for women in that the men must strive to be good enough to earn women's love. The women link love to wisdom, responsibility, and rationality. If Rose, mentioned above, is willing to dedicate herself to living for others, then the man who courts her must be good enough to earn that dedication. Consequently, the macho, rakish type stands little chance against the steadfast, stalwart type. In fact, Alcott punishes the charming but rash and impulsive Charlie with death and awards Rose to the less dashing but more deserving Mac.

The world of women and children in Alcott's stories is highly moral. The women, through their selflessness, are enshrined in a position that promises status and solidarity as rewards. The men, through the moral agency of the women, become their equivalents. The children strive to meet goals that the parents set. Since they are inherently wise and good and have the proper guidance, the goals are achievable. Together, family members form a unit that surpassed the criteria of the gentry editors of the children's periodicals who bought Alcott's work. If the purpose of the literature in the periodicals was "to excite in us the earnest purpose and humble hope so to think, to feel and to live, as not to belie our high calling,"[60] then Alcott's stories qualified.

We have seen how Alcott's short stories developed the children's moral tale as a teaching device and fulfilled the expectations of the gentry editors who published children's fiction of the day. As such, the short stories have been treated for their didactic qualities. But what of their artistic qualities? I originally read the stories hoping to rediscover some gem, a small literary masterpiece, or a characterization equivalent to that of Jo in *Little Women*. I hoped the stories would, to borrow Alcott's language, fulfill the promise Alcott shows in *Little Women*.

On the whole, the selections in the *Scrap-Bag* do not realize their promise. The quality of the collection is highly uneven, as the title suggests it might be. Some of the selections are mere

scraps—impressions, memories, sketches—obviously hasty work
that had popular salable value then as the impressions of our
best-selling authors do today. Perhaps the slightness of some of
the selections detracts from the excellence of others, yet they
are all highly readable and have a certain compelling quality
that results from Alcott's narrative ability. Among the sixty
selections there are a dozen or so stories that are very good.

The best selections in the *Scrap-Bag* are the short stories
rather than the expository pieces. They are more carefully
crafted and display the clarity and control of *Little Women*.
They are tales of children that follow the conventions of the
ordeal and change-of-heart formula, and their themes are consistent with genteel values. The conflicts involve the children
either in the display of moral integrity or the attainment of
moral perfection. Alcott's ability to characterize through narrative action raises the stories above the level of the predictable.

Because Alcott develops her stories through narrative action
—a practice that appeals to children—as opposed, say, to richly
textured description, the best stories are the longest ones. The
length allows her to develop complexities of action and subtleties of characterization that are absent in the short pieces. In
all fairness, it must be pointed out that Alcott was working
within a requirement that limited a story to around 3,000
words and that this limitation was detrimental to her stylistic
strenghts. For example, "Cupid and Chow-Chow," one of the
longest stories in the collection, is also among the best.

If there is a common subject linking the best of the stories,
it is the child in crisis. The story of the child who, for one reason or another, faces tremendous odds is the most compelling.
For example, Jack in "My Little Gentleman," a young lad who
is parentless and poverty-stricken himself, wants to bring vision
to his sightless orphan-friend Nan; and Jimmy in "Jimmy's
Cruise in the Pinafore," finds money to pay for his ill sister's
recuperation in the country. Part of the reader's pleasure is the
vicarious experience of victory that the resolution of the conflict brings. If some of the other stories are slight, it is because
the children's battles, and therefore their moral victories, are
slight. It is when Alcott explored believable extremes of the
genre that she was most successful.

The value and qualities of these short stories are difficult for
the contemporary reader to assess. For one thing, our taste in
children's literature has changed radically since the late-nine-
teenth century. Today's children seem to prefer stories that are
"real" rather than ideal. Contemporary children's literature
tends not to be didactic, although it has been said about children's literature that one generation's art is the next generation's didacticism. Alcott was writing within the conventions
of domesticity that asked for a teaching story and for the gentry editors who wanted a portrayal of the domestic ideal rather
than domestic reality. The children in popular children's fiction
today have serious human problems that they work out within
familial situations that are more characteristic of the family
that Alcott actually grew up in rather than the ones she portrayed. As Alcott did, they face egoistic parents (in her case a
father) and problems of poverty. But contemporary characters
also face the different problems that twentieth-century techno-
logical society and altered family structures and expectations
have brought about.

In *Little Women* Alcott simplified the genre of poular nineteenth-century women's fiction and directed it to a younger
audience. Her narrative ability and her rich characterizations
allowed the work to be successful, perhaps more successful
than any other novel in the women's genre of that century.
But to tell the American domestic family drama in a short story, as she did in the *Scrap-Bag* collections, she simplified the
form even more and adopted the conventions of the formula
that fulfilled the editors' expectations. That her stories succeed
to the extent they do is a tribute to her artistry.

In judging the artistic merit of her stories, we must understand Alcott's expectations of herself as a writer. Alcott's greatest artistic achievements occurred when she was still freely exploring literary forms and subjects. She hit upon success in
Little Women, and rather than reach beyond it, she contented
herself with sequels, replications, and variations. When she
moved to the genre of the children's tale, she simplified it even
more and limited herself in other ways. She committed herself
to a given number of words and a formula that governed the

story's theme, tone, and resolution. This compromise may have been an immediate advantage in that she could write such stories and still meet the numerous personal obligations that she, as "duty's child," was expected to fulfill. But, in the long run, it appears to have been detrimental. The financial exigencies that compelled her to write for short-term deadlines prevented her from creating lasting works of art.

Given her acquiescence to the conventions of the moral tale, it is fairer to judge Alcott, at least for the *Scrap-Bag* stories, most of which were written for children's periodicals, as a professional writer rather than a literary artist. In so identifying herself, she aligned herself with numerous other female writers who perceived themselves in the same way. It has been suggested that the absence of a literary masterpiece in the genre of women's fiction lies in the fact that rather than perceiving themselves as artists, these women perceived themselves as professional writers who supported themselves with meaningful writing that fulfilled an obligation to their readers.[61]

Even more profoundly, these stories may fail to move us because Alcott commits herself to a social framework that ultimately failed. As did the other proponents of the women's sphere, Alcott, at least in the *Scrap-Bag* stories, committed herself to a domestic ideal that did not realize its promise. In fact, as is discussed in chapter 4, she may have committed herself to a different course of action in the stories from that in which she believed. But, if she did, she wrote little about it, and her destruction of her diaries deprives us of any evidence. We must judge the body of prose she has given us. While the sense of sisterhood that the domestic sphere nurtured gave women status and a sense of solidarity and grouped them as a class, it did not prove to be a powerful enough social force to overcome the political and economic problems that the Gilded Age presented. In evaluating the *Scrap-Bag* selections, it is difficult to separate the failed social ideal from the fiction.

The stories are best understood as Alcott rendered them—children's tales with highly moralistic messages and didactic intentions. That they are entertaining and that Alcott perceived her work to be a valuable contribution is undeniable. It is within this conceptual framework that the analysis of the *Scrap-Bags* is undertaken. To look at them otherwise is to ignore the evidence.

NOTES

1. Edmund S. Morgan, *The Puritan Family* (New York: Harper and Row, 1966), p. 97.

2. Ibid., pp. 87-88.

3. Philippe Ariès, *Centuries of Childhood* (New York: Vintage Books, 1962), pp. 132-133.

4. A.J. Plumb, "The New World of Children in Eighteenth-Century England," *Past and Present*, 67 (May 1975), 68.

5. Bernard Wishy, *The Child and the Republic* (Philadelphia: University of Pennsylvania Press, 1972), p. 11.

6. Ibid.

7. Morgan, *The Puritan Family*, p. 45.

8. Nancy F. Cott, *The Bonds of Womanhood* (New Haven: Yale University Press, 1977), pp. 63-64.

9. Nancy F. Cott, "Notes Toward an Interpretation of Antebellum Childrearing," *The Psychohistory Review*, 6 (Spring 1978), 4.

10. Ibid.

11. Ibid., p. 5.

12. I am adopting here the major themes identified by Cott in "Antebellum Childrearing."

13. Alexis de Tocqueville, "Influence of Democracy on the Family," *Democracy in America* (New York: Washington Square Press, 1964), p. 233.

14. Cott, "Antebellum Childrearing," p. 9.

15. Wishy, *The Child and the Republic*, pp. 34-41.

16. Anne L. Kuhn, *The Mother's Role in Childhood Education* (New Haven: Yale University Press, 1947), pp. 120-148. See especially chapter 6, "Guardian of the Temple of the Immortal Soul."

17. Henan Humphrey, quoted from *Domestic Education* in Cott, "Antebellum Childrearing," p. 14.

18. Morgan, *The Puritan Family*, p. 104.

19. Peter Gregg Slater, *Children in the New England Mind* (Hamden, Conn.: Archon Books, 1977), p. 94.

20. Ibid., see chapter 3, "The Methodology of Upbringing," for a discussion of Timothy Dwight, pp. 93-127, and chapter 4, "The Structure

of Child-Rearing Theory," for a discussion of Horace Bushnell, pp. 152-164.

21. Anne Scott MacLeod, *A Moral Tale* (Hamden, Conn.: Archon Books, 1975), p. 22.

22. Ibid.

23. Louisa May Alcott, *Aunt Jo's Scrap-Bag: An Old-Fashioned Thanksgiving, Etc.*, Volume Six (Boston: Roberts Brothers, 1897), pp. 208-234. For convenience, future references to *Scrap-Bag* stories will appear in the text.

24. Heinrich Heine, "Lorelei," *Lyric Poems and Ballads*, Tr. Ernst Fiese (Pittsburgh: University of Pittsburgh Press, 1968), pp. 46-49.

25. MacLeod, *A Moral Tale*, p. 22.

26. Ibid., p. 23.

27. Samuel Goodrich, quoted in MacLeod, p. 23.

28. [Lydia Marie Child], *Evenings in New England* (Boston: Cummings, Hilbard & Co., 1824), p. 11.

29. Quoted from *The Juvenile Miscellany* in MacLeod, *A Moral Tale*, p. 27.

30. Ariès, *Centuries of Childhood*, p. 109.

31. Plumb, "Children in Eighteenth-Century England," p. 81.

32. Ibid., p. 82.

33. Ibid., p. 84.

34. Ibid., p. 85.

35. MacLeod, *A Moral Tale*, p. 40.

36. Samuel Goodrich, quoted in MacLeod, *A Moral Tale*, p. 40.

37. Nathaniel Willis, quoted in MacLeod, *A Moral Tale*, p. 19.

38. Ibid.

39. R. Gordon Kelly, *Mother Was A Lady* (Westport, Conn.: Greenwood Press, 1974), p. 5.

40. Ibid., pp. 31, 58-69.

41. Ralph Waldo Emerson, "Manners," *The Portable Emerson*, Ed. Mark Van Doren, (New York: The Viking Press, 1946), p. 168.

42. Kelly, *Mother Was A Lady*, p. 31.

43. Ibid., p. 85.

44. Ibid., p. 28.

45. Ibid., p. 35.

46. Ibid., p. 39.

47. Ibid.

48. Ibid.

49. Ibid., p. 41.

50. Ibid., p. 43.

51. Ibid.

52. Emerson, "Manners," p. 173.

53. Kelly, *Mother Was A Lady*, pp. 47-48.

54. Ibid., p. 52.

55. Ibid.

56. Carroll Smith-Rosenberg, "The Female World of Love and Ritual," *Signs*, 1 (Autumn 1975), 1-29.

57. Ednah B. Cheney, ed., *Louisa May Alcott* (Boston: Roberts Brothers, 1890), p. 15.

58. Alcott, *Rose in Bloom* (New York: Grosset and Dunlap, 1976), pp. 300-301.

59. Cott, *The Bonds of Womanhood*, p. 71.

60. Quoted from *The Living Age* in Wishy, *The Child and the Republic*, p. 54.

61. Nina Baym, *Woman's Fiction* (Ithaca, N.Y.: Cornell University Press, 1978), p. 16.

2

Alcott's Moral Code: "Making Patchwork" or "Doing the Best We Can with the Pieces Given Us"

Morality is a prominent theme in children's fiction of the early nineteenth century. Many short stories were published in Sunday school publications and serials established to teach Christian values. In her study of nineteenth-century children's literature, Anne Scott MacLeod says, "The idea of Christian morals suffused nearly all popular literature of the period and all discussion of social and political issues."[1] As we have seen in chapter 1, the major responsibility for teaching appropriate moral values lay within the home and fell to the mother. The home was the appropriate place because it represented a wholesome escape from the contradictory values and practices of the world of business and politics.

Mothers were helped in their task of teaching appropriate moral values by numerous advice books published in the early part of the nineteenth century. The authors of these books suggested that a mother could use certain works of fiction to help teach appropriate moral conduct to her children; it recommended moral tales, written largely by women and published in anthologies and periodicals of the day. In one of the best-selling advice books, *The Mother's Book*, Lydia Marie Child suggests that a few wisely chosen books could provide children with valuable lessons about life while providing a pleasant pastime. She is specific about the advantages of good reading:

> It cheers so many hours of illness and seclusion; it gives the mind something to interest itself about, instead of

the concerns of one's neighbors, and the changes of fashion; it enlarges the heart, by giving extensive views of
the world; it every day increases the points of sympathy
with an intelligent husband; and it gives a mother materials for furnishing the minds of her children.[2]

Presumably, the reading of fiction could have the same positive
effect for children that it had for adults. But children's novels
should be screened by mothers and read sparingly so as not to
diminish interest in histories, biographies, and the "old standard works."[3] Child recommends a list of books for children
that contains stories, rhymes, hymns, and lessons. She lists several works by Maria Edgeworth, saying, "Miss Edgeworth's
books are full of practical good sense, philosophic discrimination, and pure morality. They contain nothing opposed to religion, but there is an entire absence of its life-giving spirit."[4]
    Probably Child would have categorized the short fiction of
Louisa May Alcott, written several decades later, in much the
same way. Certainly Alcott approved of Edgeworth's fiction;
in Alcott's "Little Button-Rose," Miss Penny, one of the re-
spected aunts, says, "Maria Edgeworth was always a favorite
of mine, and I still think her far superior to any modern writer
for the young."[5] Alcott's fiction, like Maria Edgeworth's, is
full of good sense, philosophic discrimination, pure morality,
and there is little mention of the life-giving spirit of religion.
One of her most explicitly religious comments appears as a
conclusion to "Back Windows," a reminiscence in which she
acknowledges that our deeds follow us and speaks of a bigger
accounting at the end of life.
    The moral code that is at the heart of Alcott's short fiction
is a trinity that is spelled out in a tale called "Dandelion" (I,
91-99), a story that follows roughly the ordeal formula discussed in chapter 1. The mother, Hetty, and her three-year-
old son, called Dandelion because of his golden, fuzzy hair
that suggests a Christ-like halo, are forced to provide for themselves when Ben, the husband and father, is lost at sea. At first
Hetty will not be comforted, but eventually three "spirits"
help her deal with her loss: Love, Labor, and Hope. The spirit
of Love "took the shape of Dandelion, to comfort poor Hetty"

(93). The spirit of Labor is forced upon Hetty, who had to spin at the wheel to earn bread for Dandelion and herself. And Dandelion teaches Hetty the spirit of Hope as he hums "Daddy's tummin' soon" to the whirring of the spinning wheel. Although Hetty's faith wavers and she thinks Dandelion's hopes are in vain, Dandelion's faith is certain. And eventually,

> the bitterness of her grief passed away, and a patient hope came to her; for the child's firm faith impressed her deeply, the pious music of the sweet old hymns comforted her sore heart, and daily labor kept her cheerful, in spite of herself. The neighbors wondered at the change that came over her, but she could not explain it; and no one knew that the three good spirits, called Love, Labor, and Hope, were working their pleasant miracles. (96)

Six months later, Ben returns to an aged but cheerfully resigned wife and son, "who had not forgotten his father" and whose faith had brought him home.

A closer look at the *Scrap-Bags* reveals that the moral code of Love, Labor, and Hope which enabled Hetty and Dandelion to survive is at the heart of relationships among characters and provides the motivation for their behavior. In the case of "Dandelion" Love is that of mother-and-son, but in other stories, it is simply the love of one human for another—of brother and sister, friend and stranger, white and black, and rich and poor. Labor in "Dandelion" is motivated by need, but in the other stories, Labor is its own reward. It is clear that ordinary labor at humble tasks is dignified and noble and that there is satisfaction in doing well those tasks that, for one reason or another, we must perform. One of the prominent themes in this category is that it is especially important to labor in some positive way if one is wealthy. And finally, with Hope, given Love and Labor, one cannot fail. This hope appears to be a faithful optimism, an intuitive sense that in a well-ordered world, good will prevail.

Although this moral code operates at the heart of all the stories in the *Scrap-Bags*, it is stated explicitly in only one other story, "Marjorie's Three Gifts" (IV, 144-160). Here the basic trinity remains the same; only in this case the "spirits" are "gifts" and presented in a different order: Industry, Cheerfulness, and Love. It is significant that these stories were originally published seven years apart—"Dandelion" as "The Little Boats" in 1869 and "Marjorie's Three Gifts" as "Marjorie's Birthday Gifts" in 1876—representing a consistency of theme over an important period of time. By 1869 Alcott had sold dozens of stories to periodicals for over ten years and had published several collections of children's short stories. In 1868 she began a brief stint as editor of *Merry's Museum*, during which she developed a sense of editors' expectations for what the short stories should say. By 1876 she was at the height of her career, the most memorable of her works had been published, and only fourteen more of her *Scrap-Bag* stories remained to be written.

"Marjorie's Three Gifts" opens as Marjorie, a poor girl who lives with her grandmother, daydreams of receiving three birthday gifts—a good-luck penny, a talisman to keep her always happy, and a prince with a kingdom over which to reign. However, the gifts Marjorie receives differ from those of which she has dreamed. She is taught the value of the three-part moral code through three separate experiences. She willingly and cheerfully helps an old, lame man care for his frisky pony and receives a gold coin for her kindness, along with a lesson: "Industry is a good teacher, and money cannot buy happiness, as I know to my sorrow" (148). Next, Marjorie returns a floppy white hat, which has blown away, to a young lady who gives her in return a lovely picture and teaches her a lesson of optimism: "Just believe that there is a sunny side to everything, and try to find it, and you will be surprised to see how bright the world will seem, and how cheerful you will be able to keep your little self" (154). Finally, her friend Billy brings her a garland of daisies for her hair and organizes a party of her friends, who love Marjorie because she is "sweet and good." Marjorie assesses the gifts happily—her bank with the gold coin represents the good-luck penny, the picture is her talisman to keep her always happy, and the daisy crown of flowers is given by Billy, her friend and "prince." The moon that shines in her window knows that the gifts represent "three good spirits [that] had come to help little Marjorie from that day forth, and their names were Industry, Cheerfulness, and Love" (160).

In nearly all of the other stories in the collections, the characters and conflicts grow out of a belief in the three-part code, although, in most cases, while demonstrating the code implicitly, they deal with only one or two of the "spirits" explicitly. Here the "spirits" are dealt with in the order in which they are emphasized in the collection. Although the themes are closely intertwined, usually one tenet of the moral code predominates. Alcott speaks most frequently and emphatically of the importance of labor, followed by love, and, finally, by hope.

THE VALUE OF LABOR, OR "ALL HAVE THE CHOICE TO WEAR OUT OR RUST OUT"

In a collection of stories following the tradition of the moral tale and the prescriptions of the gentry editors' social code, one expects a predominance of moral lessons to guide children on the path to a successful life. The most surprising element one discovers in exploring the stories in the *Scrap-Bags* is Alcott's primary moral lesson that happiness is found through industriousness.

The discipline of labor and its implications for living are best spelled out in "Patty's Patchwork" (I, 193-215), a story written for the first volume of the *Scrap-Bags*, which introduces the dominant metaphor for the collection. The story builds around the experience of ten-year-old Patty, who is visiting her Aunt Pen while her mother awaits the birth of a child. Soon after Patty's arrival, Aunt Pen proposes that Patty make a comforter for the new baby. But it is clear to Aunt Pen the "comforter" has several meanings and will teach Patty "something better even that the good old-fashioned accomplishment of needlework" (196). (In *The Mother's Book*, Child recommends making patchwork as "sufficient employment" for children. She says, "Making patchwork . . . is a quiet amusement; and if a child be taught to fit it herself, it may be made really useful. If the corners are not fitted exactly, or the sewing done neatly, it should be taken to pieces and fitted again; for it is by inattention to these little things that habits of carelessness are formed."[6])

Making an analogy to life, Aunt Pen proposes the comforter be a "moral bed quilt" that has "patience, perseverance, good nature, and industry" sewn into it. She says to Patty, "Our lives are patchwork, and it depends on us a good deal how the bright and dark bits get put together so that the whole is neat, pretty, and useful when it is done" (194). The quilt becomes a sort of diary, reflecting Patty's moods—her happiness at befriending the poor, crippled neighbor girl, and her guilt at accidentally pulling the tail feathers from the pet canary or intentionally taking a bun without telling her aunt. Patty understands that she is "making two kinds of patchwork at the same time" and that the handwork in the quilt is symbolic of the lessons of life. As Aunt Pen says,

> Every task, no matter how small or homely, that gets well and cheerfully done, is a fine thing; and the sooner we learn to use up the dark and bright bits (the pleasures and pains, the cares and duties) into a cheerful, useful life, the sooner we become real comforters, and every one likes to cuddle about us. (196-197)

Thus, the sewing hour becomes a conscience hour, and the moral lesson is clear and acceptable to both Patty and the reader. Moreover, the point is reinforced, in a way that to the modern reader seems unnecessarily cruel, when Aunt Pen tells Patty that her new baby sister has died several days after birth. Although Patty grieves and does not want to continue the quilt, Alcott stresses the necessity for the discipline of labor by having Aunt Pen insist that Patty continue to work on it: "Mamma will love to see it, so I wouldn't give it up. Work is the best cure for sorrow; and I think you never will be sorry you tried it. Let us put a bright bit of submission with this dark trouble, and work both into your little life as patiently as we can, deary" (207). With trembling hands and quivering lips, Patty proceeds to sew, each day confronting her grief through her work. Finally, when Patty is called home, Aunt Pen finishes the quilt by sewing a star in the middle and adding several moral poems for the lessons Patty has learned. She concludes:

> The goods and the bads got into the bed-quilt in spite of you, and there they are to tell their own story. . . . It is just so with our lives, though we don't see it quite as clearly as this. Invisible hands paint our faults and virtues, and by and by we have to see them, so we must be careful that they are good and lovely, and we are not ashamed to let the eyes that love us best read there the history of our lives. (214-215)

By recognizing the value of the project, Patty is able to become her mother's comforter. Alcott is saying that through work we can come to terms with life's grief. The stress is on the work, not only for the necessity of it, but also for the solace it can bring. Although other Alcott stories deal with poverty-stricken people or those who have recently fallen from wealth or those who must devote themselves to the care of others, in this story—which makes the value of work so clear—there is no need to labor for monetary gain or to care for another. It is simply that work is good and can have a healing effect.

Alcott deals with the value of work in different ways for different social classes. For the wealthy, the principle is not to waste one's life on silly social customs and time-consuming frivolities. Rather, the well-to-do should do their duty by using their talents to help the less fortunate. This point is clearly made in two fables published in the *Scrap-Bags*.

We have already discussed "A Curious Call" (I, 111-122), a fable that personifies the statues of Boston. In that story, the golden eagle from the City Hall visits the narrator ("a literary woman of Boston") and admonishes her to write stories that help people understand they should not be "so wrapped up in their own affairs" but rather look about for something to do (121). Work is closely associated with doing one's duty, which appears to mean working with the gifts one has been given. Alcott makes the point again in another fable, "What Becomes of the Pins" (V, 188-208). The story is told by plain Granny

Pin, who recounts her life of service to an actress, a dying man,
a soldier, and an escaping female slave. The wealthy mistress,
Miss Ellen, in whose pincushion Granny resides, overhears the
adventures and realizes she is wasting her life on frivolities, doing nothing in a world full of work. She resolves "to choose
the right way in time, and wear out with doing our duty, rather
than rust out as so many do" (207).

It is not only to the wealthy that Alcott directs her message.
The lesson of labor is directed to the poor as well, who often
teach the wealthy through example. In "Fairy Pinafores" (III,
91-114), Cinderella's godmother builds a home for a group of
poor, sick, helpless orphans and teaches them the need for
cleanliness, a love of nature, and—most important— the value
of labor. She instructs them in the art of pinafore-making,
teaching them "to employ their hands, make them happy, and
be of use to others" (98). The pinafores, though out of fashion,
are sensible and comfortable. The poor girls sell the pinafores
(which gain a magic quality from the love and good will put
into them) to the rich girls of the town, who have a change of
heart when they put them on, and miraculously turn from selfish to loving. The rich children convert their parents, who eventually convert the king, queen, prince, and his Cinderella. And
everyone lives happily ever after, knowing that useful labor
will give meaning to their lives and guarantee their happiness.

In still another story the poor teach the rich the value of
labor. In "Roses and Forget-Me-Nots" (IV, 64-86), a wealthy
young girl, significantly named Belle, learns the value of labor
from a poor decorative flower maker. Lizzie saves the day for
Belle when she creates the perfect garland for Belle's hair, an
ornament that will beautifully complete her costume for the
dance. Belle remembers Lizzie as an errand girl who many
years earlier had delivered a hat. Belle discovers that Lizzie is
crippled, yet content, for she has her work. Belle says to Lizzie, "I feel so idle and wicked when I see busy people like you
that I reproach myself for neglecting my duty and having more
than my share of happiness" (81). And she resolves to work by
carrying out "precious little deeds of love and sympathy" that
are "strong to bless, . . . easy to perform, [and] . . . comfortable to recall" (83).

3. "Promise that I may make the flowers you wear on your wedding-
day," whispered Lizzie, kissing the hand held out to help her rise.
"Roses and Forget-Me-Nots," *My Girls, Etc.*, Vol. 4.

Perhaps the strongest testimony to the dignity of honest labor occurs in a story whose characters are adults, thus emphasizing the lesson of labor for grown-ups as well. In "What A Shovel Did" (V, 154-167), Richard, a young, starving writer, is near despair and considering suicide when he spies a young lad shoveling snow. He suddenly realizes that he can use his muscles, if not his brains, to earn his way: "As I live I *will* try it! and not give up while there is any honest work for these hands to do" (156).

After shoveling snow for a wealthy family, Richard hears a marvelous tale from a household maid, which he weaves into a story and sells. He continues working and writing and eventually the woman he left when he decided to devote himself to writing discovers him. Because he is struggling so humbly at his labor, she gives him her love, saying, "Richard, I was afraid you had gone down as so many disappointed young men go when their ambitious hopes fail; but I am glad, so proud to see in your face that you still work and wait, like a brave and honest man" (165). Eventually they marry, and Richard's wife hopes their sons will "inherit not only their father's respect for honest work, but the genius that can see and point to truth and beauty in the humble things of this world" (167). Alcott explicitly states that one can resort to physical strength and labor when all else fails. Physical labor, she says, is noble: if one is willing to work, no matter how menial the task, success will come, along with the precious ability to see truth in humble things.

Alcott repeats this message again and again. In "Tessa's Surprises" (I, 35-57), twelve-year-old Tessa Bennari is responsible for caring for three younger brothers and sisters after their mother's death while their father, an immigrant Italian, works as a plasterer. She decides she will buy Christmas gifts for the children: "I must earn the money; there is no one to give it to me, and I cannot beg. But what can I do, so small and stupid and shy as I am? I must find some way to give the little ones a nice Christmas. I *must!* I *must!*" (37). At this point a splendid idea comes to Tessa: she will sing for money with her orphan friend Tommo, who makes his living by playing the harp in the streets for money. Even though it is cold and few people pay to hear their music, Tommo and Tessa determinedly continue their work. When the pair is nearly ready to give up, Alcott rewards them for their efforts. The children of a wealthy family give them money, food, clothes, and an invitation to join in their Christmas celebration.

The theme of work in Alcott runs through her longer fiction as well. *Little Women* opens with the four March sisters grumbling about their poverty. By the end of the novel, the girls assume a certain nobility because Marmee has taught them to take pride in humble work. Meg and Jo support the family when their father is away at war, and Marmee constantly helps poor neighbors. But Alcott gives the subject of labor the fullest treatment in the novel *Work, A Story of Experience*, completed in 1873. The title page of the novel quotes Thomas Carlyle: "An endless significance lies in work; in idleness alone is there perpetual despair."

Work records the experiences of Christie Devon as she sets out on her own to find support, happiness, and a home for herself. Not bound by a family to whom she is responsible, Christie leaves her aunt's home on the farm, where she faces only "everlasting work, with no object but money. I can't starve my soul for the sake of my body, and I mean to get out of the treadmill if I can. . . . I'm willing to work, but I want work that I can put my heart into, and feel that it does me good, no matter how hard it is."[7] Alcott tells the reader Christie's goal will be difficult; how she realizes it gives us insight into how she perceives the role of work in women's lives.

Alcott was aware of the changes in women's roles from the beginning of the century to 1873, when she finished the novel. During that time women's roles had changed from direct power and equal participator in labor and decision-making in a family to indirect power through the separate sphere of home and family. As Sarah Elbert points out in the introduction to her recent edition of *Work*, Alcott had argued in her earlier writing that "young women were incapable of sensible child care if they were excluded from education and employment in the larger society."[8] In *Work* Alcott shows a woman's struggle for indivi-

4. ''Sing, Tessa, Sing!'' cried Tommo, twanging away with all his might. ''Tessa's Surprises,'' *My Boys, Etc.*, Vol. 1 (illustration from *Shawl-Straps*, Vol. 2).

dual fulfillment through employment in the "larger society."

Christie Devon places her faith in a wage system that will reward her efforts. But in successive jobs—as servant, actress, governess, companion, and seamstress—Christie discovers that work does not fulfill the promise of independence she envisioned. As Christie finds, the personal service occupations are humiliating because of the prescribed social relations: "Even in democratic America, the hand that earns its daily bread must wear some talent, name, or honor as an ornament before it is very cordially shaken by those who wear white gloves." Alcott is quick to point out—probably she experienced it herself—that class distinctions became polarized, and the "lady" becomes elevated to a high social status. The common laborer could not hope to reach it without some "talent, name, or honor."

And, of course, Christie has none of these. Eventually, when penniless, jobless, and considering suicide, Christie meets Cynthie Wilkins, who befriends her and introduces her to a group of reformers. She eventually marries one of them, but he soon dies in the war. Christie continues her devotion to reform work, especially for the cause of working women. At a women's rally, she stops at the bottom step of the platform, saying, "I am better here, thank you; for I have been and mean to be a working woman all my life." Christie realizes that women must not accept the evils of the wage system. She, as Alcott did, vows to continue to care for her family through joining various women's reform groups. She says, "I owe all I can do, for in labor, and the efforts and experiences that grew out of it, I have found independence, education, happiness, and religion."[9] Her message becomes more emphatic when we realize that she was saying this at the time when idleness for women had become a status symbol, especially in the upper middle class. Thorstein Veblen commented that by the end of the century it was almost the sole function of the upper-middle-class lady to provide evidence of her husband's wealth.[10] Chapter 4 shows Alcott's disapproval of such a role.

The model of gaining significance through work that Alcott quotes from Carlyle was surely provided by her own family. Her father, Bronson Alcott, is remembered as a thinker and

talker and therefore not as a worker. However, he was seldom,
if ever, idle. Because he refused to work at supporting his family in a traditional way, because he experienced what at the
time were spectacular failures, and because his daughter was
therefore forced to support the family, today Bronson tends to
be associated with idleness.[11] Nothing could be farther from the
truth. As Madelon Bedell has pointed out in her recent biography of the Alcotts, Bronson worked constantly. He wrote

> no less than sixty-one volumes of journals, some of them
> containing more than a thousand pages, ten volumes of
> "Autobiographical Collections," in which he pasted clip-
> pings, advertisements, photographs, letters, maps, pamph-
> lets, and other documents relating to his life and times;
> forty-one volumes of letters to and from himself and his
> family; and thirty volumes of mostly unpublished works.[12]

He was constantly occupied with reading, recording the activities of his daughters as they grew, writing, teaching, and travel-
ing and "conversing" on a public speaking circuit. His constant
labor provided an important message about the value of work.

Louisa's mother was also devoted to labor. The novel *Work*
is dedicated "To My Mother, whose life has been a long labor
of love." Abba reared four children, supervised a home (often
without help) that she moved literally dozens of times, entertained Bronson's guests, wrote frequently herself, and in fact
occasionally worked outside the home to support the family.

Louisa's mother came from the distinguished New England
May family and her father, from a New England farm family.
Surely both families had been nourished in the Calvinistic ethic
that called for a commitment to creating evidence of an active,
successful, serious, work-filled life to relieve the insecurity and
to provide evidence of one's propensity for salvation. Louisa
herself worked continuously; Bronson called her "Duty's Faithful Child" and continually reminded her of her obligations to
duty, conscience, and the family. Alma J. Payne writes, "To
maintain the family became the dominant duty of her life, and

she tried the accepted feminine occupations: teaching, sewing, even domestic service, where she was forced to fend off the unwelcome attentions of her minister-employer. Only her pen gave promise of supporting [them]."[13] In time, Louisa's duty led her to support and care for three families: her parents; her nephews (after her sister's husband, John Pratt, died); and her niece, Lulu Nieriker (after her sister May died). Even on her first trip to Europe, which might normally be perceived as a holiday, she was employed as a companion to a young, sickly woman. In fact, as critics are fond of pointing out, Louisa died only several days after her father, realizing that, finally, her duty to her family had been fulfilled.

The lessons about duty and work that Bronson Alcott taught Louisa, using metaphors from *Pilgrim's Progress* which she later adopted as chapter titles in *Little Women*, were passed on in the stories she wrote for children. Many of her stories are primarily devoted to showing children the virtues and rewards of work. She assumed the genteel manners and values that her editors insisted her stories teach were correct; she knew how many people were impoverished, and she wanted them to understand that all work is noble.

The period of Alcott's life witnessed great changes in the role of working women. The women who went to work in the textile industry in the early 1800s had relatively high wages, respectability, and status. But as the decades passed, the nature of the labor force changed and so did the wages, status, and respect of the women. It also witnessed great changes in the working status of children. Joseph F. Kett argues in *Rites of Passage* that by 1840, for all practical purposes, the true apprenticeship for boys had declined, and machine technology had made the apprenticeship nothing more than machine tending.[14] Girls were still entering the work force in various capacities. Alcott knew that many of her readers, both female and male, were either holding jobs or soon would, and she was eager to remind them of the dignity of their labor. She was also a forerunner in pointing out the value of education in helping one attain work goals; by the end of the century, children were encouraged to finish high school, perhaps even to add an additional year or two be-

yond that to their education to avoid the dead-end jobs that
technology created.

THE VALUE OF LOVE, OR "DO AS YOU'D BE DONE BY"

The second "spirit" or "gift" in the three-part moral code is
love, shown most frequently in the form of one person com-
forting another, as Dandelion comforts his mother when she
grieves for her husband, who is lost at sea. In many cases those
in need of love are family members, but the spirit also operates
as merely the pleasure of doing good for another, being kind to
another, or sharing. Often the ones "doing good" are nearly destitute themselves. As Mother says to Tilly in "Tilly's Christmas,"
the pleasure of doing good is "one of the sweetest things in life,
and the poor can enjoy it as well as the rich" (I, 130). Those
who give love have the power to transform the lives of others
and thereby their own. As we have already pointed out in chapter 1, one of the criteria in the gentry code is to serve those
poorer and more helpless than oneself.

By linking love to the pleasure of doing good, Alcott links
that love inexorably to the "spirit" of work. Doing good for
others is working for them, or caring for them, or serving them
to ward off poverty, illness, or even death. Often the love is offered at the expense of great self-denial and self-sacrifice, especially when the ones who are giving and loving are poverty-strick-
en themselves. Alcott's message is that those who help are poor
in money but rich in love. This love for humankind is often sig-
nified, as it was in the writing of so many of the other nineteenth-century women, by a love of flowers. The titles of several
of Alcott's collections of stories suggest the theme of love:
Flower Fables, her first collection; *Morning Glories;* and *A
Garland for Girls*, published in 1887 when Alcott was near
death.

The majority of stories that deal with the value of love portray characters living in poverty, nearly starving, ill, or approaching death. Often the children are either orphans or have only
one living parent—usually a mother—making the ordeal they
face even more difficult. Of the sixty stories in the *Scrap-Bags*,

fourteen have protagonists who are orphans; by no coincidence these stories deal primarily with the value of love and labor. Another nine stories, which explore similar themes, tell of children with only one living parent.

In "Patty's Place" (IV, 161-186), Alcott explores the power of love to transform. Patty, a thirteen-year-old who is pale, short, disfigured, and shy, lives in an asylum for orphans. Often overlooked by those who come to the asylum seeking servants, she despairingly longs for someone to recognize her capable and gentle ways. Patty is encouraged by a visitor, Miss Murray, who advises her to seek friends and fortune for herself "by taking cheerfully whatever comes, by being helpful and affectionate to all, and wasting no time in dreaming about what may happen, but bravely making each day a comfort and a pleasure to yourself and others" (167).

Eventually Miss Murray recommends Patty to her brother's family, and Patty serves the Murrays for a year, working capably and following the advice of her benefactor. However, no one shows her any special kindnesses or love, and she pours out her sorrow in letters to her friend. The Christmas holiday (holidays are *always* a festive occasion in Alcott's fiction, as they were in the Alcott household) presents the opportunity for Miss Murray to teach the family a lesson of love. She reads them Patty's letters, and they guiltily recognize their wrongs. As Alcott says, "It is astonishing how generous and kind people are when once waked up to a duty, a charity, or a wrong" (179). The family plans special kindnesses for Patty, but mostly they demonstrate they care. Their love transforms her to a smiling, confident, bright-faced girl, for whom service is no longer a burden. Happy with her situation, Patty claims "There is no finer fortune than love."

It is interesting that Alcott should choose such a setting to tell a story about the power of love. In the fiction by nineteenth-century female authors, a woman in a servant role is almost never portrayed as a heroine.[15] We have already seen how Alcott explores a similar theme, portraying Christie Devon in *Work* as realizing that it is not the little pay that is the problem, but rather the social attitudes that make the positions of servitude unacceptable. Alcott published "Patty's Place" in *Young*

Folk's Journal in January and February 1874, only a few
months after the publication of *Work* in 1873.[16] Her journals
indicate that she objected to such attitudes in her own experience as a domestic. By choosing an unlikely setting and an unusual relationship among characters, Alcott makes her point
about the power of love to transform more telling.

Some of Alcott's best stories with similar themes follow
roughly the ordeal formula described earlier. In most of these
stories the ordeal is resolved through some type of labor, thus
uniting the themes of labor and love. One of the best stories
following the ordeal formula is the title story of volume five of
the *Scrap-Bag*, "Jimmy's Cruise in the Pinafore" (V, 5-26),
which Alcott was inspired to write after seeing a production of
H.M.S. Pinafore. Jimmy's burden is that his sister, Kitty, is ill;
his mother has been told by the doctor that Kitty must have
country air to recover from her fever. As the author explains,
"There was no father to lend a strong hand, and Mrs. Nelson
was one of the 'silent poor,' who cannot ask for charity, no
matter how much they may need it" (7). Twelve-year-old Jimmy tries in vain to earn money for the trip. When Jimmy's
best friend, Willy Bryant (a young neighbor girl) enters with
the suggestion that they audition for children's roles in a local
production of *H.M.S. Pinafore*, the problem is resolved. Jimmy
and Willy audition successfully. Through his love and willingness to work, Jimmy is able to send Kitty and his mother to
the country with his wages of ten dollars a week.

Another twelve-year-old boy who helps others and is rewarded by his labor is Jack Floyd in "My Little Gentleman" (I, 134-
147). Nearly destitute himself, Jack carries market packages or
clean clothes, sells chips, and grubs in the ash-heaps for cinders,
hoping to earn enough money to provide for an operation for
his orphan friend Nanny, who has "a white film slowly coming
over her pretty blue eyes" (135). Fortunately, while digging
through an ash-heap, Jack finds an old pocketbook with fifty
dollars in it. Alcott adds a moral lesson by having Jack adver-
tise for its owner, but virtue is rewarded and no one claims the
money. Foregoing all the things he dearly needed and wanted
for himself, Jack takes Nanny to Dr. Wilkinson, who restores
Nanny's sight and, impressed by Jack's honesty, willingness to

5. Dolly opened the door, and started back with a cry of astonishment at the lovely spectable before her. "How It All Happened," *An Old-Fashioned Thanksgiving*, Vol. 6.

work, self-denial, and love for Nanny, takes him on as an errand boy. Jack soon finds "that many comforts quietly got
into his life; that much help was given without words; and that
the days of hunger and rags, heavy burdens and dusty ash-heaps,
were gone by forever" (146).

In "How It All Happened" (VI, 37-52) Alcott contrives the
setting so that a neighbor, Miss Kent, overhears through the
thin walls of the boardinghouse two young girls bemoaning
their poverty, particularly their lack of money and gifts to celebrate Christmas: "It does seem as if rich people might think
of poor people now and then. Such little bits of things would
make us happy, and it couldn't be much trouble. . . ." (39-40).
Although Miss Kent is only a milliner and not rich, as the innocent girls perceive her to be, she plans special gifts and inspires
others in the boardinghouse to do the same. They all find that
"kind deeds often come back to the givers in fairer shapes than
they go" (46). In fact, Miss Kent's loving nature captivates Mr.
Chrome, one of the boarders. They fall in love and thus illustrate a moral lesson: "You see, when people once begin to do
kindnesses, it is so easy and pleasant they find it hard to leave
off; and sometimes it beautifies them so that they find they
love one another very much" (48-49).

As with the theme of work, Alcott makes a point about the
power of love by giving life to inanimate objects or animals
and having them tell a tale. In "Autobiography of an Omnibus"
(IV, 187-204), the omnibus, who tells the story of his life, feels
his greatest achievement is in providing a temporary home for
the poverty-stricken Schmidt family. (Apparently this story is
based on an actual incident; Alcott published an earlier version
as a true-life account.[17]) The family lives in the omnibus during
the mild months until twelve-year-old Hans can find work in a
factory to support his mother and sisters. Eventually the factory
workers learn of the Schmidts' plight and have the opportunity
to show their love by helping the Schmidts find permanent
housing.

In other tales of love, Alcott draws from real experience, as
she did in "Autobiography of an Omnibus." In these narratives,
she speaks directly to the audience. In what appears to be a personal reminiscence from her European trip, Alcott narrates the

tale of "Little Marie of Lehon" (I, 158-175). Marie, the daughter of poor French parents, brings fresh goat's milk to the travellers. A charming, loving girl, she entertains the travellers with French tales of love and sacrifice that foreshadow her own heroic actions. Marie saves an old, disfigured, nearly insane woman from starving by secretly watering her vegetable garden. For this secret and loving charity, which awakens both the villagers and the travellers to the value of doing good for one another, little Marie is publicly praised and blessed by the local priest.

Alcott is obviously touched by and wants to share with her audience the examples she has known of poor, young children who are forced to earn their way for themselves and sometimes for their friends and families as well. In another personal reminiscence, "Our Little Newsboy" (I, 186-192), Alcott discovers Jack Hill, a nine-year-old newsboy who has been pushed aside by older newsboys and forced to sell late at night: "Such a little fellow as he was, in the big, ragged coat, such a tired, baby face, under the fuzzy cap, such a purple, little hand, still holding fast a few papers; such a pathetic sight altogether, was the boy, lying on the stone step, with the snow drifting over him, that it was impossible to go by" (186). Fearing he will freeze, Alcott buys his papers, feeds him, and tells his story, hoping that "when busy fathers hurry home at night," they will never pass feeble, shabby or hungry-looking newsboys without buying a paper. She instructs: "For love of the little sons and daughters safe at home, say a kind work, buy a paper, even if you don't want it; and never pass by, leaving them to sleep forgotten in the streets at midnight, with no pillow but a stone, no coverlet but the pitiless snow, and not even a tender-hearted robin to drop leaves over them" (192).

The spirit of love is at the heart of the message in *Little Women* as well. The message that Marmee teaches Meg, Jo, Beth, and Amy is to think of others first. In the first chapters of *Little Women*, Marmee encourages the girls to give their Christmas breakfast to poor neighbors. With some effort, all learn the lesson of love. Jo learns to deny herself in order to do good for others so well that she ultimately devotes her life to others. In *Little Men*, Jo, with her husband, Professor Bhaer, establishes Plumfield, a school for problem boys.

As Jo devoted her life to rehabilitating problem children at Plumfield, Louisa too devoted herself to others, primarily her family. As a child her mother taught her with three simple instructions she never lost sight of, neither in her life nor in her stories: "Rule yourself. Love your neighbor. Do the duty which lies nearest you."[18] Her devotion was total: she worked for her family when she would have preferred to write and when she was ill herself. This commitment meant supporting them financially, since Bronson refused to accept that traditional responsibility; it meant caring for them when they were ill; it meant cleaning the house and preparing the food when no one else could; it meant finding housing for them when, for one reason or another, the old place became unacceptable. Is it any wonder that love became so closely linked to work and duty for Alcott? And that love and labor became consistently treated themes throughout her fiction?

THE VALUE OF HOPE

The third "spirit" or "gift" in the moral code, hope, is roughly equivalent to optimism. In one of the stories in which Alcott spells out the moral code, she calls the third gift "cheerfulness," explaining it as similar to hope. As labor and love are intertwined, so hope is linked with labor and love. Alcott says that if people work industriously and show their love by doing good for others, they are justified in hoping for the best. If labor and love do not bring success, a cheerful, faithful hope will finally win the day. Sometimes the line between cheerful optimism and wishful thinking is slim.

Although Alcott thinks of love in the western Christian sense of "doing unto others," her presentation of hope is not necessarily religiously linked. In both of the stories where she spells out the moral code most explicitly she avoids the use of the word faith, the concept that was at the heart of Puritan's labor and love. Occasionally she relates hope and cheerfulness to a general faith that the Supreme Being will reward, but the greater emphasis is on faith in one's self. As a child of twelve, Louisa had written sample lessons in her journal in which she attempted to define hope. The sequence reads:

Write a sentence about anything. "I hope it will rain: the garden needs it."

What are the elements of *hope*? "Expectation, desire, faith."

What are the elements in *wish*? "Desire."

What is the difference between faith and hope? "Faith can believe without seeing; hope is not sure, but tries to have faith when it desires."[19]

Tilly in "Tilly's Christmas" (I, 123-133) illustrates the nature of cheerful optimism, tinged with a hint of uncertainty that relates it to hope rather than faith. Tilly is trudging home from school with several friends who speak with anticipation of the Christmas holiday and the presents it will bring. Tilly is eager too, although she knows she will receive no presents. As they talk of Christmas, Tilly spies an injured bird, which she takes home to nurse. Her friends chide her for this silliness, reminding her, "He can't pay you for taking care of him, and my mother says it isn't worth while to help folks that can't help us" (126). Tilly replies that her mother's favorite maxims are "Do as you'd be done by" and "Love your neighbor as yourself." And she adds optimistically, "This bird is my neighbor, and I'll love and care for him, as I often wish our rich neighbor would love and care for us" (127). Tilly's friends depart, teasing her for her wishful thinking. Tilly muses, "Never mind, birdie, we'll make the best of what we have, and be merry in spite of everything. . . . And I know God won't forget us, if every one else does" (128).

Alcott rewards Tilly's kindness and hope. Using a favorite device, she introduces a wealthy neighbor who has, by coincidence, been present and overheard Tilly's conversations with her friends and mother. The neighbor anonymously produces the gifts Tilly had hoped for, thus reinforcing the moral lesson that kindness and hope are rewarded, in this case by an act of charity.

In reviewing the characters in the stories discussed earlier in the chapter who reveal this quality of hope or cheerfulness, one discovers that the hope is coupled with a determination to make events work out, even if the character has no apparent means of bringing about the desired outcome. As Tessa in "Tessa's Surprises" (I, 35-57) says, "I *must* find some way to give the little ones a nice Christmas. I *must!* I *must!*" (37). Jimmy in "Jimmy's Cruise in the Pinafore" (V, 5-26) says of his sister's need to get to the country, "She *shall* go! I don't see any other way, and I'll do it" (8). Jack in "My Little Gentleman" (I, 134-147) is cheerfully optimistic, in spite of the fact that his dear friend Nanny is losing her vision, "This was Jack's great trouble, and he couldn't whistle it away as he did his own worries; for he was a cheery lad, and when the baskets were heavy, the way long, the weather bitter cold, his poor clothes in rags, or his stomach empty, he just whistled, and somehow things seemed to get right" (135). As days pass and Nanny's vision worsens, Jack visits a doctor and is turned away by his nurse because he has no money; he resolves, "I'll get the money somehow, and *make* him let me in" (137).

In the stories nearly all the children involved in some personal ordeal are determindedly hopeful. In seeking to understand the optimistic outlook of so many of the children in Alcott's short stories, one is reminded of Louisa's father, Bronson, and his attitudes toward children and their education, attitudes that he must certainly have conveyed to his daughter. As his diaries and observations of his daughter show, Bronson believed in the child as an "innocent messenger from the world of the spirit, possessing intuition and insight into the real nature of things,"[20] a view which was radically different from that of most New Englanders in the early part of the nineteenth century. This perception of children leads naturally to a cheerful optimism about the possibilities and alternatives that are available to them. From his writings, we know these possibilities are reflected both in his childrearing and his teaching, particularly at Temple School. Alcott "used Christian vocabulary, yet spoke of radical dependence on the self" and he "praised fiction for presenting moral truths not clearly illustrated in daily life, and celebrated the imagination as a guide in fixing habits of thought and feeling."[21]

During the years when Louisa was most impressionable, Bronson was at the height of this optimism. He was glorying in his friendship with Emerson and the other more formally

educated ministers and thinkers of the Transcendentalist Club.
And he was developing the ideas and curriculum for the most
successful educational venture of his life—Temple School. He
was additionally hopeful because during this time Abba was
pregnant with what Bronson hoped would be his first son. He
writes to his mother:

> I am full of hope, and everything looks encouraging.
> As to money, that you know, is one of the last of my
> anxieties. I have many friends, and am making more daily,
> and have only to be true to my principles, to get not only
> a useful name, but bread and shelter, and raiment. . . .
> I am still the same Hoper that I have always been. Hope
> crowned me while I was following the plow on the barren
> and rocky fields of that same farm on which you now
> dwell, and Hope will never desert me either on this or the
> other side of the grave.
> I fancy that I was quickened and born in Hope, and
> Hope in the form of a kind and smiling mother, nursed
> me, rocked my cradle, and encouraged my aspirations,
> while, I was the child, and the youth, seeking life and
> light amidst the scenes of my native hills. Those visits to
> libraries; those scribblings on the floor; those hours given
> to reading and study, at night or noon, or rainy-day; and
> even those solitary wanderings over southern lands, were
> this same Hope seeking to realize its highest objects. My
> grandfather was a Hoper; my mother inherited the old
> sentiment. . . .[22]

Further, he was at this time devoted to observing, recording,
and shaping the behavior of his daughters—Alcott recorded five
volumes of "Observations" on his children. Louisa was problematical and Bronson particularly devoted himself to understanding her. Because of this burden, Bronson spent a great deal
of time with her; his messages of self-control, of insistence
that she could accomplish whatever she wished, of faith in her
ability to overcome problems made a strong impression.

Louisa certainly remembered the quality of hope and faith
that her mother, Abby Alcott, demonstrated so often. Abby

wrote the following note to twelve-year-old Louisa in her journal: "My Dearest Lorry,—I often peep into your diary, hoping
to see some record of more happy days. 'Hope and keep busy,'
dear daughter, and in all perlexity or trouble come freely to
your Mother."[23] The Alcott's biographer Madelon Bedell says
that Abby's "sustaining rock was her faith in her husband."
She quotes an example of such faith: "'I believe my husband
will be my Savior,' she declared, 'for he has brought a clearer
revelation to my mind of the will of God, destiny of man, and
purpose of life, than any minister I ever heard of or any Bible
I have ever read.' "[24]

In case the reader is tempted to dismiss the importance of
the third part of Alcott's moral code as merely childish optimism appropriate for youngsters, it is necessary to look at how
pervasive positive idealism was in mid-nineteenth century America. William James, writing at the end of the nineteenth century,
recognized it, called it the "religion of healthy-mindedness,"
and devoted a chapter to it in his study of human nature called
The Varieties of Religious Experience. James explained that
happiness characterizes the believers in such a "religion," as it
does the children in Alcott's stories. James describes such believers as "those who, when unhappiness is offered them, posi-
tively refuse to feel it, as if it were something mean and wrong.
We find such persons in every age, passionately flinging themselves upon their sense of the goodness of life, in spite of the
hardships of their own condition, and in spite of the sinister
theologies into which they may be born. From the outset their
religion is one of union with the divine."[25] That characterization reminds us of Tilly, who says, "Never mind, . . . we'll make
the best of what we have and be merry in spite of everything"
(I, 128). And Tessa, who says, "I *must* find some way to give
the little ones a nice Christmas" (I, 37). James would include
such people in the concept of the "once-born," which is characterized by a "childlike nature" that causes them to be optimistic and not fearful of God, who to them is kind and beautiful. As James explained, this attitude tempers their perception
of sin: "Of human sin they know perhaps little in their own
hearts and not very much in the world; and human suffering
does but melt them to tenderness. Thus, when they approach

God, no inward disturbance ensues; and without being as yet spiritual, they have a certain complacency and perhaps romantic sense of excitement in their simple worship."[26]

Theodore Parker and Ralph Waldo Emerson are mentioned by James as proponents of the "once-born" family of healthy-minded religion. Both, of course, were members of the Transcendentalist Club, contributors to *The Dial*, and frequent visitors to the Alcott home. Both refused to dwell on the darker aspects of life and emphasized the positive, idealistic side. Emerson became the foremost spokesman for transcendentalism, which was based on "a glorification of the imagination, the beauties of nature, the wisdom of the child, the essential goodness of the human being," and above all "the spirit of optimism and faith in the progress of humanity."[27] In Emerson's essay "Nature" he writes, "Who can set bounds to the possibilities of man?"

Louisa adopted these idealistic transcendental notions in the *Scrap-Bag* stories. Her wise children could count on the goodness of others to assure their success against improbable odds. She wrote the first of her short stories for Emerson's children when she was experiencing what she later referred to as a sentimental infatuation with him. During this time, she sought opportunities to be near him, reading in his library, listening to his talks, teaching his children, and entertaining them with her stories. What better way to flatter him than to create stories that reflected his ideological beliefs! These early stories embodied a basic tenet of transcendentalism—the spirit of optimism and faith in the progress of humanity. Once that perception of humankind was established in her stories, she never departed from it. Many years later, writing in *Rose in Bloom*, Alcott has her heroine return to Emerson and his essay "Self Reliance" to find inspiration for her proper place in life.

If the incurable optimism was limiting to Alcott, it was a problem she shared equally with Emerson and other transcendentalists. But Alcott capitalized on "the religion of healthy-mindedness," integrated it into her fiction as the value of hope, wedded it to the doctrine of work in the Protestant ethic and the doctrine of love in Calvinism, and thereby established her moral code.

THE BURDEN OF THE MORAL CODE

In reviewing the stories in the *Scrap-Bags* and studying their
themes, the reader is struck with their seriousness. The message
and burden was awesome: Labor, Love, and Hope. From the beginning, Puritans had placed great responsibility on their children. In the Puritan notion, children were sinful; they were
formally educated to ensure their religious welfare, ultimately
to ensure salvation. Their behavior was expected, as part of the
family covenant, to provide evidence of their love (and fear) of
God.

The stress in Alcott's code on the child's obligations to labor
and love are remarkably similar to those of "moderate" persuasion described by Philip Greven in *The Protestant Temperament*.
As Labor (often connected with duty, as we have seen) is dominant over Love in the Alcott stories, so "Duty was of even greater significance [than love] as a motif of the moderate temperament and religious experience."[28] Children in such families
grew up with a sense of free will, but they understood the limits
that the term "duty" imposed on their freedom. Their duty,
usually balanced by a sense of love, suggested subordination,
deference, and respect.

This deference to duty that characterizes the self-controlled
moderates described in Greven's book is developed in Alcott's
stories through the sense of obligation that binds family members together. Children are obligated to parents, grandparents,
and siblings. They follow certain rules of decorum, usually
taught by their mothers, in carrying out their duty. Their reward is often only the love of the parent or sibling who bene-
fitted from their kindness, which, of course, often serves to increase their sense of obligation. The children in the stories are
faithful to their duties, understanding somehow the fulfillment
of their obligations is shaping their character. While creating
demanding restraints on them, the duties, performed out of
love, ensure that no child is ever alone. Even orphan Jack
develops a series of relationships through his obligations to
duty that bind him to a wider system of support, in his case,
the physician who begins to take care of him.

The burden for children in Alcott's stories is great because her expectations for them are great. The motivation to work solely for the love of God that the early Puritans had stressed is gone. Alcott's religion provides a general framework of meaning to life's experiences. There is a force watching over the characters in her stories, yet salvation isn't their point. The emphasis is on laboring and loving as ends in themselves rather than for the salvation they will bring.

Only the hoping, the cheerfulness, is not for its own sake. One has the feeling that the children are encouraged to be cheerful because the burdens of labor and love are so difficult. In stories with love as the theme, the love should bring joy; but the emphasis is that love represents the burden of labor, as it did in Alcott's life. The child is always the giver, the doer. Of course, the children are rewarded, but so often the rewards are fleeting. The Bennaris in "Tessa's Surprises" (I, 35-37) get a bit of food, a few cast-off clothes, and the chance to participate in a wealthy, healthy family's Christmas celebration; the day after Christmas they must again face their poverty. Even the wealthy people are made to feel guilty for their idleness. For them true happiness can come only from serving others.

The moral code called out serious responsibilities for the children of the 1860s, 1870s, and 1880s. The goal they were to seek appeared to be perfection. As we shall see in the next chapters, Bronson Alcott wanted the education of his daughters to be an "experiment in perfecting mankind." Because the childrearing practices of her father had been so successfully integrated as part of her own value system and because that value system coincided so well with the requirements of the editors who published her stories, this notion of striving for perfection pervades them. It also has important implications for both the behavior she expected from children and her perception of them.

NOTES

1. Anne Scott MacLeod, *A Moral Tale* (Hamden, Conn.: Archon Books, 1975), p. 28.

2. [Lydia Marie] Child, *The Mother's Book* (New York: Arno Press and The New York Times, 1972), p. 86.

3. Ibid., p. 95.

4. Ibid., p. 100.

5. Alcott, *A Garland for Girls* (New York: Grosset and Dunlap, 1977), p. 212.

6. Child, *The Mother's Book*, p. 61.

7. Alcott, *Work* (New York: Schocken Books, 1977), p. 9.

8. Ibid., p. xxiv.

9. Ibid., p. 442.

10. Thorstein Veblen, *The Theory of the Leisure Class* (New York: New American Library, 1953). See, for example, the chapter "Dress as an Expression of the Pecuniary Culture," pp. 118-131.

11. Carol Gay has argued that Bronson has been maligned by his daughter Louisa's misunderstanding and contempt of him, in part for not contributing financial support to the family. While I accept that Louisa's public posture called to everyone's attention that Bronson contributed little to the family coffers, it does not necessarily follow that Louisa misunderstood her father or intentionally maligned him—or that she had the inability to mature. "The Philosopher and His Daughters," *Essays in Literature, Western Illinois University*, 2 (1975), 181-191.

12. Madelon Bedell, *The Alcotts* (New York: Clarkson N. Potter, Inc., 1980), p. 335.

13. Alma J. Payne, "Duty's Child," *American Literary Realism, 1870-1910*, 6, no. 3 (Summer 1973), 260-261.

14. Joseph F. Kett, *Rites Of Passage* (New York: Basic Books, Inc., 1977), pp. 145-152.

15. Nina Baym, *Woman's Fiction* (Ithaca, New York: Cornell University Press, 1978), p. 69.

16. "Bibliography" in Madeleine B. Stern, *Louisa May Alcott* (Norman: University of Oklahoma Press, 1950), p. 352.

17. Ibid., p. 347.

18. Ednah D. Cheney, ed., *Louisa May Alcott* (Boston: Roberts Brothers, 1890), p. 57.

19. Ibid., p. 43.

20. Bruce Allen Ronda, "The Transcendental Child," Ph.D. Dissertation, Yale University, 1975, p. 86.

21. Ibid., p. 100.

22. Richard L. Hernstadt, ed. *The Letters of A. Bronson Alcott* (Ames, Iowa: The Iowa State University Press, 1969), p. 41.

23. Cheney, *Louisa May Alcott*, p. 42.

24. Abby Alcott, quoted in Bedell, *The Alcotts*, p. 42.

25. William James, *The Varieties of Religious Experience* (New York: Mentor Books, 1958), p. 77.

26. Ibid., p. 78.

27. Bedell, *The Alcotts*, p. 112.

28. Philip Greven, *The Protestant Temperament* (New York: Alfred A. Knopf, 1977), p. 178.

3

The Promise of Youth

It is not surprising that when Louisa May Alcott began writing short stories she turned to children as the subjects and audience for her fiction and to the promise of youth as her major theme. Her father, Bronson, can properly be called America's first child psychologist. Bronson had a way with children that led him to a career in teaching; his wife, Abigail, supported his passion for the study of children. He devoted much of his life to what he thought would be an experiment in perfecting humankind—the rearing and teaching of children—and took his daughters as the specials subjects of his study. Although he recorded voluminous notes on the developmental progress of all four of his daughters, his two eldest, Anna and Louisa, served as models for his most complete case studies. He wanted to overcome traditional child-rearing methods and replace them with innovative ones that complemented his assumptions of the child as innocent and wise. His notes record his hopes for the experiment:

> We do not yet know . . . what favorable influences, from birth, will do for the infant. . . . It is reserved for some individual, who . . . shall take the infant, from the beginning, and paying due respect to his whole nature, shall cooperate with it, in due accordance and harmony with the laws of its constitution, and suggest to the world, both by success and failure, what the human being may become.[1]

His experiment began in 1831 with the birth of his daughter Anna and the beginning of his record, "Observations on the

Phenomena of Life, as Developed in the Progressive History of an Infant, during the First Year of its Existence." The birth of Louisa in 1832 introduced an interesting variable, and he began to record his observations of Louisa's development, as well as his observations of the interactions of the sisters and the problems with parental discipline that sibling rivalry precipitated. Perhaps Louisa's obsession with the subject of children can be traced to the serious conversations that she had with her father as he was trying to discipline her and thereby shape her character. He expected nothing less than moral perfection in his children, and Louisa was problematical from the beginning.

Bronson's expectations were probably not unreasonable, given his beliefs about the nature of the child. For Bronson, as for Emerson and the other transcendentalists, the child was a symbol of the promise of humankind—simple, innocent, and idealistic. He opposed the prevalent Calvinistic doctrine that the infant was depraved by the taint of original sin. He called himself a "signer-off from Calvin's colder creed" and in 1831 wrote in his journal:

> Of all the impious doctrines which the dark imagination of man ever conceived, this is the worst. This is, indeed, the sin, which is unpardonable—the belief in the original and certain depravity of infant nature. If man had set himself down to contrive an agency which would . . . most effectually degrade human nature, he could not have accomplished his foul purpose so effectually as by this. Happy is it for the world that the progress of our race has outdistanced this debasing doctrine; that nobler views are gaining currency. Infancy is beginning to be respected.[2]

Bronson worried about the effect that the notion of infant depravity would have on parents' handling of their children and feared a "self-fulfilling prophecy," and he wrote in his observations, "Having made the child perverse by inheritance, ye contrive, upon principle, to make him so by education."[3]

Bronson took his duties as a parent very seriously. Much more than most fathers of the day, he insisted in playing an important role in the rearing of his daughters, a task that his vocation as writer and teacher enabled him to do. In order to develop the strong bond of affection that he believed to be the basis of parent-child relationships, he spent a lot of time with his children. He thought seriously about the implications of their behavior and his reactions to it. He wanted his daughters to be protected from fear, punishment, and coercion. He appealed to their sense of voluntary control over willfulness and their sense of reason, believing that the best "punishment" was the withholding of parental approval. He and his wife, Abigail, were to be exemplary models for their daughters.

From the beginning, Louisa was a difficult child—obstinate and aggressive—who severely taxed her parents' patience and childrearing plans. Abigail responded by occasionally resorting to spanking. In these instances Bronson speculated that mother and daughter were much alike. He summoned all the patience, gentleness, and affection he could muster and proceeded to reason with his daughter, reinforcing her good behavior with praise and affection and punishing her naughty behavior by withholding affection and sometimes isolating her. His major tactic was to play on her conscience. His journal records Socratic-like question-and-answer sessions designed to reveal her naughty behavior and to develop her sense of duty to herself and others.

There is no doubt that Bronson succeeded in developing her sense of conscience.[4] Not only did he engender in her a perception of herself as duty's child, but also he gave her the perception of the child as wise. Although there is some evidence that Louisa dismissed some of her father's more radical notions, she embraced wholeheartedly his notions on the nature and education of children. In fact, the childrearing and educational theories behind Jo's practices as head of Plumfield in *Little Men* and *Jo's Boys* are none other than those Bronson practiced as a teacher at Temple School and as the parent of his own daughters.[5]

It is important to remember how different Bronson Alcott's notions of children were from the prevalent views of the day. Alcott characterized children as innocent nearly seventy years befor G. Stanley Hall celebrated the child in *Adolescence* (1904) and John Dewey described progressive education based on the child's experience in *The School and Society* (1899). Bronson was one of the first to question the notion of infant depravity, still widely held among those of "evangelical" persuasion in the early nineteenth century. Others whom the Alcotts knew also questioned it. For instance, Lydia Marie Child described the child in *The Mother's Book* in 1831, the same year that Bronson began his "Observations," as a "little image of God" newly arrived from heaven, an act that has been called unprecedented.[6] She writes, "They come to us from heaven, with their little souls full of innocence and peace; and, as far as possible, a mother's influence should not interfere with the influence of angels."[7]

Bronson's views of the perception of children were equally unprecedented. Many of them were shared by the transcendentalists; some of his notions were more extreme. All transcendentalists saw children as being in touch with the real meaning in life and filled with wonder, fresh perceptions, and the uncanny ability to speak the truth. They had been influenced in their perception of children by the romantics Coleridge and Wordsworth. Many of the transcendentalists had read Wordsworth's "Ode: Intimations of Immortality From Recollections of Early Childhood" as "a celebration of the child's intuitive contact with the divine, and a call for adults to return to that kind of immediacy."[8]

Like Bronson, the transcendentalist Ralph Waldo Emerson held the child in high regard, referring throughout his writing to the "genius" of childhood. In "Education" he argues that we should have "men whose manhood is only a continuation of their boyhood, natural characters still," explaining that boys naturally know truth from falsehood, can detect weakness in character and behavior, and respond with candor and honesty. He continues: "They make no mistakes, have no pedantry, but entire belief on experience. Their elections at baseball or cricket are founded on merit, and are right. They can't pass for swimmers until they can swim, nor for stroke-oar until they can row: and I desire to be saved from their contempt. If I can pass with them, I can manage well enough with their fathers."[9]

While Emerson and the other transcendentalists argued for the genius of children, Bronson Alcott was willing to go one step farther and argue that adults could learn from the wisdom of children, who possessed intuition and insight into the real nature of things. It is for this reason that he devoted so much of his life to the study and education of children.

Education was important because it was a quest to recover the intuitive knowledge of childhood. Education had to be appropriately designed to recover this knowledge. In his attempts to recover this intuitive knowledge, Bronson often parted company with the other educators of the day because his approaches were different. The school in which the child was to learn must have a pleasant, comfortable, healthful environment (this meant individual chairs, with back supports). Play, physical education, and activities were important, too, as a close relationship existed between the development of mental ability and physical activity. Like other educators who were to come later, he believed the curriculum should be developed from the experiences of the child and utilize the awareness and trust of the senses that children possess. It should encourage self-reliance and allow opportunities for social contacts. Students were taught to balance their selfish personal interests against those of society by developing self-discipline and control.

Because self-discipline and control were so important, Bronson placed a great emphasis on moral education and character building. For this he cultivated the development of conscience by teaching self-control, "submission of the body in favor of the spirit." Alcott explains that by reaching the child's will and subduing desires he could control the child: "I shall first remove obstructions to the growth of the mind: these lie in the appetites, passion, desires, and will. Intellectual results will follow the discipline of sentiments; for in these lie the guiding energies of the whole being."[10] Many of his lessons were devoted to the internalization of moral truths and duties. To this end he encouraged introspection and the development of the imagination, believing it had been the guiding impulse of society. Genius, which had shaped the common mind, was nothing more than imagination in action. One of the ways to stimulate and develop the imagination was through study of literature. It has been suggested that Alcott's perception of the imagination as a way of cutting one free from conventional language and interpretation, and his insistence that his students press beyond literal meanings, especially of religious events and beliefs, led, in part, to the closing of Temple School.[11]

If Bronson as educator was eventually prohibited from stimulating the imagination of his students, Bronson as parent was not prevented from stimulating the imaginations of his daughters. They were encouraged to write stories and plays, which they dramatized for family and friends, with each of the daughters assuming various roles. Later it was Bronson who insisted to Louisa that there was a market for such a book as *Little Women*.

When Louisa began to write, it was natural for her to create her characters engaged in conflicts and exhibiting behavior that was consistent with the beliefs in which she was nurtured. Those around her were transcendentalists, and from the beginning her characterization of children reflected transcendental notions. Some of her first stories, written for Emerson's children, embodied many of his attitudes toward nature and children. They also reflect the love of nature that Thoreau communicated to her during the years that he was very friendly with Bronson and played with Louisa and her sisters on various outings. But mostly they reflect her father's beliefs.

Again and again, her stories portray children as full of wisdom and intuitive knowing. In the ordeal stories, their ability to accomplish so much is due, not to genius, but to their willingness to trust hunches; their superior moral strength and character coupled with the discipline of self-control inevitably yield success. The most prominent and consistent characterization, based most certainly on one of Bronson's fundamental notions, is of the child as teacher. The thematic concerns that emerge deal with the proper education of children: in many cases, through their "intuitive knowing," children suggest educational innovations. As Bronson was concerned with teaching reforms, concerns for health through nutrition, physical exercise, comfortable dress, and enjoyment of nature, so Louisa adopts these as subjects in her *Scrap-Bag* stories. The magazines in which she originally published them offered a perfect forum for spreading the gospel of the child that she had come to believe.

THE CASE FOR CONSCIENCE IN THE DEVELOPMENT OF CHILDREN

In Alcott's stories a strong conscience guides the children to intuitive knowing. For Bronson, the spirit functioned within the individual as conscience, suggesting a clear link between social behavior and understanding of the spirit. He explains, "I observe that those who cannot conceive of spirit without body, existing in God before it comes out upon the earth, are the very ones who have required the most discipline and punishment, and have the least love of obedience. The rest are those who exercise most self-control, and seem to have the most conscience."[12]

Following her father's philosophy, Louisa writes stories that portray children guided by their conscience. The story that illustrates most explicitly the role of conscience in developing a strong character has the conscience assume the shape of a shadow to guide development. In "Shadow-Children" (VI, 104-123), the conscience—(Bronson would have called it a "spirit")—takes the form of each child's shadow and disengages itself from the child in order to teach proper behavior. The shadow, in effect, is an alter-ego that acts as a conscience.

The story is unique in that the shadow-consciences are not directed by an adult. They know intuitively what the proper behavior is and guide the children to it by modeling the behavior themselves. In "Shadow-Children" three young children—Ned, Polly, and Will—sit one morning on the steps "wishing they had something pleasant to do." They have been given chores by their mother, but choose to neglect them. The fantasy of the shadow as alter ego is introduced when Ned says, "I wish my shadow wouldn't mock me. Every time I stretch or gape it does the same, and I don't like it" (104). Polly and Ned agree it would be fun to see their shadows "cut capers," and in a quick transition from reality to fantasy, the shadows come to life: "three little shadows on the sunny wall behind them stood up straight, and began to bow" (105). A soft voice instructs the children that the shadows will remain if the children promise to follow them and to tell no one else of their existence.

Through the vehicle of the morning chores, each of the shadows teaches the child proper behavior. Ned's shadow takes him to the garden and his task of picking peas. When Ned objects, the conscience "communicates" to Ned (there is never any direct dialogue—the message arrives to each child intuitively through the modeling of the shadow) and brings about his insight: "Oh! you mean that she does lots for me; so I ought to do what I can for her, and love her dearly" (106). The insight causes a change of heart and Ned joins his alter ego, the shadow, in carrying out the task. Both Polly and Will's experiences follow a similar pattern. The afternoon excursion to the woods allows the childrens' shadows to teach them proper judgment: Ned realizes the foolishness of venturing across the rapids in a leaky boat; Polly befriends a little lame girl; and young Will resists the temptation to disturb baby birds and to eat poisonous berries. In gratitude, Will thanks his shadow, "Good little shadow, to keep me safe! . . . I like you; and I'll mind better next time, 'cause you are always right" (118). With the direction of the three shadows, the children arrive home safely and promptly for late afternoon tea.

An indirect association to the mother as the inspiration and teacher of the shadows is introduced in the story's final scene. At bedtime, it becomes clear that their mother is the inspiration for what the shadows do. As the mother is preparing the children for sleep, her shadow emerges to sing a good-night lullaby, supporting the behavior of the shadows that the children followed. As they fall asleep, the children acknowledge the lessons that their shadows/consciences taught them. Ned says, "It's been a good day, and I'm glad we tried our wish; for the shadows showed us, as well as they could, what we ought to do and be. I shan't forget it, shall you?" Polly confirms that she is "much obliged for the lesson," and Will concurs, saying, "I shall be very careful where I lead my shadow, 'cause he's a good little one, and set me a righter zarmple than ever I did him" (123). The story concludes with the children resolving as they fall asleep that "their shadows should not be ashamed of them."

Bronson would have approved of Louisa's use of her literary imagination and her choice of subject matter. As he said, imagination is "the power whereby you picture out thoughts that never were realized in the world."[13] Here Louisa conceptualizes the conscience in the form of a shadow that attaches itself to a child and, instead of mimicking his or her behavior, directs it. In doing so, it models proper behavior, which includes respect for parents, acknowledgment and acceptance of responsibility, love and kindness to both family and friends, and concern for the welfare of animals. Since, in fact, the child and the shadow are one, the reader assumes that the children, through their consciences, intuitively knew the right behavior. This conceptualization of shadow as after ego anticipates the notion of personality as being divided into separate functions that Sigmund Freud was to advance later. Like Freud's notion of "superego," Alcott's conceptualization of conscience develops in response to the rewards and punishment meted out by parents.

The minor conflicts in her stories occur when temptations try to override conscience to lead the children astray. As Bronson had taught his students and his daughters, the secret to overcoming temptations is through self-control. The major conflict of Louisa's counterpart in *Little Women* centers on her battle to control her impetuous temper. Like her literary counterpart, Louisa struggled with the same conflict, especially in her early years, as her father's journals so poignantly show.

Louisa's father would have argued that this task of getting the conscience to control behavior is relatively easy because children are innately wise. Their education is merely to help them retain, and if necessary, to recover, the innate wisdom of their childhood. That is why Ned in "Shadow-Children" arrives so easily at the moment of insight that tells him what to do and why to do it.

Most of the children in Alcott's stories possess a sense of intuitive knowing that allows them to bring wisdom to their handling of interpersonal relationships. This sense enables them to work well with people and sometimes to accomplish things that adults, who fail to listen to their consciences and who have lost their sense of intuitive knowing, cannot accomplish. For this reason, children often assume the role of teacher. As Bronson thought that adults could learn from children, so Louisa structured her stories to show that they do. We have seen how their consciences enhance their wisdom; now let us turn to how children use their wisdom to teach.

CHILDREN AS TEACHERS

The children in Alcott's short stories often stand in judgment of what they perceive to be the failures of the adults in their lives. The conflict of many of the *Scrap-Bag* stories involves a child's attempt to correct the errors of adults. As these are stories of domestic situations, the adults who benefit from the children's lessons are often family members—parents, aunts and uncles, and older siblings.

We have already considered several of the stories that show children as teachers. Occasionally children learn what to teach through dreams. In other stories, they simply intuit or imagine the solution. In "The Children's Joke" (I, 67-90), the Fairbairne children idly speculate that their parents would understand the unreasonable restrictions imposed on them if only their parents had to assume the children's roles. The idea of role-playing—a fairly sophisticated and popular contemporary solution for understanding and empathizing with another—is born. The role-playing idea meets with immediate reinforcement from Aunt Betsey and a willingness to cooperate from their parents. And through the agency of the children's scheme, the parents realize their errors. (An early reviewer thought "serious-minded parents" might object to this story.[14])

In "Nelly's Hospital" (III, 55-80), Nelly's love of and respect for nature brings about her brother's recovery and teaches her friends to love nature. Nelly has observed her mother caring for her brother Will, who has been injured in the war, and decides she wants to build a little hospital to care for injured animals: "For, loving all little creatures as she did, it grieved her to have any harm befall even the least or plainest of them." With the aid of the gardener's son Tony, Nelly sets up her little hospital

He prayeth best, who loveth best,
All things both great & small i
For the dear God who loveth us,
He made and loveth all!

6. ''Nelly's Hospital,'' *Cupid and Chow-Chow, Etc.*, Vol. 3.

in a summerhouse and learns through watching Tony and reading books how to care for injured animals. Her sensitivity and
concern for the animals' injuries rekindles an interest in living
for her brother, whose "cheerful courage which led him safely
through many dangers seemed to have deserted him, and he
was often gloomy, sad, or fretful" (62). He eventually leaves
his bed to help his sister with her hobby: "Every evening
brother Will read aloud to her from useful books, showed her
wonders with his microscope, or prescribed remedies for the
patients, whom he soon knew by name and took much interest
in" (77). Finally, the healing power of nature and the love and
gentle prodding of his sister for "all things, both great and
small" bring about his recovery. In addition, Nelly's hobby
causes "rough lads [to look] ashamed when in her wards they
found harmless creatures hurt by them." Though Nelly is on
holiday, she has learned as much from observing nature as she
could from books and formal schooling.

The children in the *Scrap-Bag* stories do not limit their
teaching of adults to family members. In their naiveté they also
take on those whose superior education prevents them from
being in touch with their intuitive selves. Since intuitive knowledge brings great happiness, they are kept from the most important joys of life. Like Nelly in "Nelly's Hospital," Bertie in
"Little Neighbors" (IV, 116-143) has a great love of animals.
Bertie wants to learn how to communicate with the birds that
hop about on his porch and so visits a neighbor, Professor Par-
patharges Patterson, to see if "bird language was among the
seven" he knew. While listening to the boy chatter about the
birds, "the ghost of a smile began to flicker over his lips, and
peer out from behind his glasses, as if somewhere about him
there was a heart that tried to welcome the little guest, who
came tapping at the long-closed door" (123-124). When the
professor admits he cannot help the young boy, Bertie responds,
"You must have been a *very* idle man to live among books till
you are gray, and not know a simple thing like this" (124).

Accepting the challenge, the Professor pulls out his Audubon
collection and thus begins the development of a relationship in
which the Professor learns as much from Bertie as the child
does from him. Through the sharing of their mutual interest,

which the Professor had long forgotten, Bertie changes Professor Patterson from a dreary recluse to a loving, happy man. Through Bertie he is able to bring his life into balance, using his talent to compose and illustrate a beautiful children's bird book. Alcott is suggesting, through the character of Professor Patterson, who willingly and happily puts aside his studies of "dead" languages to participate in Bertie's interests, that caring for people is the most important work one can do. The relationship is two-way: Bertie learns from the Professor about the birds, and the Professor learns from the child what Alcott would call the lesson of love.

All these intelligent children help those around them by teaching what they know of the most effective way to live. This knowledge is derived from their intuitive selves (we have seen how this knowledge is related to the "spirit" of conscience) and their experience, however brief it may be, with the tenets of the moral code—love, labor, and hope. Obviously, due to their youth, they cannot teach theory or particulars. The children don't teach "book-learning," although they are interested in it; instead they teach attitudes and perspectives. Ultimately, their message centers around learning regard for fellow human beings and creating successful interpersonal relationships.

Alcott's children insist that people are more important than possessions or needless social rituals. Their general rule is the golden rule. They will not tolerate half-heartedness; they demand that adults dedicate themselves seriously to answering their questions. They are especially good at making adults see things from the point of view of others and making them understand how their thoughtlessness and disregard is hurting others. The Fairbairne children help their parents realize their unreasonable demands, and Bertie helps Professor Patterson realize he has buried himself in his books to escape loneliness.

How do the children teach? Louisa's father often argued that teaching by example was the most effective way. What Louisa capitalized on in her stories was that teaching by example could work two ways: adults can also learn from the example of children. Children are in touch with the feelings of others and unabashedly admit the importance of loving and being loved. In some cases their youth allows them to pose questions that would be unacceptable for adults to ask. Bertie can say to Professor Patterson, "You must have been a *very* idle man to live among books till you are gray, and not know a simple thing like this" (IV, 124). The naive and innocent eye of youth sees immediately the truth and recognizes what is important in relationships.

PROBLEM CHILDREN

The intuitively wise children in Alcott's *Scrap-Bag* stories are indeed remarkable. But what about the children who are less than perfect—the mischievous, the naughty, the disobedient? Are all of the children good? And all of the time?

The answer to these questions becomes clearer if we look at the types of children portrayed in nineteenth-century fiction. The most prominent is the saintly child who is potentially perfect, who, in spite of her or his valiant effort of "labor, love and hope" of the moral code, realizes she or he still has great lengths to go in order to become perfect. Such children are all very much a part of the ordinary, hearty, day-to-day workings of this world, not at all the fragile, ethereal types that are characteristic of the unequivocally saintly.[15]

Given the basic assumption of the child as wise, with which Alcott begins, it is only consistent for her to create characters whose major conflicts involve attaining their potential perfection. Having perfection nearly within their grasp and understanding what they are doing, they try to teach others, including adults and even scholars, how to attain it. In fact, such characterizations of the children in the *Scrap-Bag* stories suggest two subcategories of the potentially perfect—first, those who are striving for themselves, and, secondly, those who, understanding their struggle, try to give other children (and adults) the faith and determination to become perfect themselves. So, indeed, children who at the outset of the story are naughty and disobedient are, by the conclusion, close to realizing their potential perfectability. As a result, the children of the *Scrap-Bag* stories are remembered as saints and not sinners. This is because the change-of-heart stories are success stories: the children who follow the formula of the moral code inevitably suc-

ceed in striving for moral perfection and in helping others attain
it also.

How is it that the children are so successful? Does their wisdom and intelligence, coupled with their devotion to the moral
code, guarantee success? Or do none of the children truly en-
counter evil? Since the children are innately good, the stories
of conscience present no struggle with evil, being cast in the
tradition of healthy-mindedness and positive thinking.

What are some of the problems, other than struggles of conscience, that the children in the stories confront? Because they
are drawn in settings of domestic crisis, they never confront
the evils of the marketplace or political arena. In the stories of
social issues, the culprit is the rigid and senseless customs imposed by the social set. In the personal stories, the antagonist
tends to be internalized, the victory is one of will. In reviewing
the *Scrap-Bag* stories, other than those which expose the social
customs of the well-to-do, we see the children confronting two
basic, often related, problems. One frequent problem is that
either one or both of their parents are dead, which often brings
about a second problem—poverty.

Alcott was always sensitive to the needs of the "silent poor."
Her memories of a youth of poverty allowed her to create sensitive and accurate characterizations of poor children. When she
was a successful author, she often gave money to needy acquaintances as "a thank offering for my success." She explains: "I
like to help the class of 'silent poor' to which we have belonged
for so many years,—needy, but respectable, and forgotten because too proud to beg. Work difficult to find for such people,
and life made very hard for want of a little money to ease the
necessary needs."[16]

In the case of orphans and children of single-parent families,
the children accept their fate matter-of-factly and try to make
the best of the situation. The moral code is their salvation. As
we have seen in chapter 2, although their burdens may be difficult, they manage to cope. All succeed if they are persistent.
Their love for humankind and cheerful, hopeful manner con-
vince skeptics; eventually they meet their goal, fleeting though
it may be, to earn enough money to pay for medicine or a gift
that represents a temporary respite from their dreary poverty.

In spite of the fact that nearly all of the stories are of saintly children, there is a suggestion now and then that the naughty child appealed to Alcott. She tells us so in "Back Windows" (I, 148-157), a personal narrative that is a categorization of the lives that "an inquisitive old lady" views through the back windows of her home. In this narrative, Alcott describes people as they "really are," taking "a look at . . . the shady side which we don't show the world, seeing the trouble, vanities, and sins which we think no one knows" (156). The girls are introduced in a way that suggests their predictability—they "have tea-parties, make calls, and play mother, of course." But the boys are more interesting: three of the nine pages are devoted to boys— "bless their buttons!—how amusing they are" (151). And over one full page describes the antics of a naughty rascal who obviously attracts the narrator. She writes, "I know I ought to frown upon this reprehensible young person, and morally close my eyes to his pranks; but I really can't do it, and am afraid I find this little black sheep the most interesting of the flock" (154).

Perhaps this attraction is typical of that which Leslie Fiedler describes of the Good Bad Boy that is so prevalent—and such a contrast of the Good Good Girl—in our literature, the Tom Sawyers and Huck Finns that the Becky Thatchers and Aunt Pollys are fated to love so much.[17] Like them, Alcott has a personal attraction to willfulness, having memories, perhaps, of the behavior problem she presented to her parents. As we have noted, Bronson's journals reflect again and again the difficulties he had in disciplining her, and Bronson makes clear his belief that Louisa took some small satisfaction in the difficulties she caused.

One of the most charming pieces in the *Scrap-Bags* is "Poppy's Pranks" (VI, 124-146), the record of the close calls of "thoughtless and curious" Poppy, a Good Bad Girl. The narrative is autobiographical, a fact the reader immediately suspects, due to the fondness and authority with which Alcott recounts Poppy's pranks.[18] Poppy spoils new shoes, wanders off and gets lost, is punished by being tied to the arm of a sofa for a full day, but continues her naughtiness—eating tobacco, breaking the jelly jar, cutting her hair, and playing in the barn where she steps, barefoot, on a pitchfork. At the age of eight, "she got so very wild that no one could manage her but mamma" (140). Because mamma is ill, she is sent to stay with grandpa, where her misbehavior continues. Eventually, she returns home, "much to her delight and much to mamma's also." Alcott concludes by reminding us that mothers love both good and bad children, "for no matter where she went, or how naughty she was, mamma was always glad to see the little wanderer back, and to forgive and forget all Poppy's pranks" (146).

"Poppy's Pranks" was originally included in *Morning-Glories and Other Stories*, which was copyrighted in 1867 and published in 1868, months before *Little Women*. Poppy's willfulness is very similar to Jo's. It is the convincing and authoritative characterization of Jo's struggle to control her temper, emotions, and desires that makes *Little Women* great. And Jo's great empathy for the curious, willful, and disobedient leads her to teach problem boys at Plumfield in *Little Men* and *Jo's Boys*.

Apparently Louisa learned the same lesson of control that the naughty children in her stories did and believed in the importance of it enough to make it a dominant subject of her stories. There are a few stories, however, that suggest she enjoyed rebelling. For example, she wrote a group of "thrillers" that Madeleine Stern has collected in *Behind a Mask* and *Plots and Counterplots* with themes and subjects of manipulating heroines and heroes, mind control, opium addiction, gothic romance and devices, Italianate Englishmen, madness, and hashish experimentation.[19] She was writing the sinister stories of forceful, independent, sexually demanding women at the same time she was writing the children's stories. But she remembered her father's lessons of conscience and, given the opportunity to publish in magazines that she knew were to shape the moral behavior of children, she disregarded the subject of evil and told domestic tales of wise children following a tough moral code that promised satisfaction.

THE EDUCATION AND CARE OF CHILDREN

How were these wise, intuitive children to be properly nurtured and educated to realize the promise of their youth? The *Scrap-Bag* stories offer no explicit formula. With the exception of a single story, they are not stories of schoolchildren. The single exception of "My Little Schoolgirl" records a little girl's friendship with the author; school is relevant only in that the author's encounters with the girl occur when she is on her way to school. There are no schoolroom scenes, as there are in *Little Women* and *Little Men*, from which we can deduce Alcott's notions of education. But we can make some assumptions about how and from what and whom children learn. First of all, the ultimate purpose of education is a moral one, as we have already seen from Alcott's emphasis on the moral code. Education is for the purpose of knowing the difference between right and wrong. Here she agreed with Emerson, who wrote: "The great object of Education should be commensurate with the object of life. It should be a moral one; to teach self-trust: to inspire the youthful man with an interest in himself; with a curiosity touching his own nature; to acquaint him with the resources of his mind, and to teach him that there is all his strength, and to inflame him with a piety towards the Grand Mind in which he lives."[20] Like Emerson, Alcott's *Scrap-Bag* stories suggest that the moral instruction should not "swallow up all the other instincts and faculties of man." Education should take the child and develop his potential "in the very direction in which it points."

Like her father and her friend Emerson, Alcott believes that the best lessons come from the direct experience of the child. The opportunities first present themselves in the home, and as we shall see in chapter 4, the mother is the first and best teacher. The most effective way to approach lessons in living and learning is by setting a good example, as all the child-rearing experts had been saying since the beginning of the century. The trick is to develop and nurture the natural interests of the child. Emerson said it this way: "Nature, when she sends a new mind into the world, fills it beforehand with a desire for that which she wishes it to know and do. Let us wait and see what is this new creation, of what new organ the great Spirit had need when it incarnated this new Will."[21]

It is also clear that education is an open experience, not confined merely to the knowledge one gets in books or schools. Once again, Alcott clearly agreed with Emerson, who said,

"Education should be as broad as man. Whatever elements are in him that should foster and address."[22] Since so much emphasis is placed on following the child's natual interests, it follows that some of the major lessons of life come from one's natural surroundings.

In a final way, Alcott is similar to Emerson and her father. She insists on respect for the child. It is apparent again and again that the education and nurturance of children is one of the most important activities one can be engaged in. By listening carefully to the child, the teacher will know how to proceed. "The secret of Education," wrote Emerson, "lies in respecting the pupil." He continues:

> It is not for you to choose what he shall know, what he shall do. It is chosen and foreordained, and he only holds the key to his own secret. By your tampering and thwarting and too much governing he may be hindered from his end and kept out of his own. Respect the child. Wait and see the new product of Nature. Nature loves analogies, but not repetitions. Respect the child. Be not too much his parent. Trespass not on his solitude.[23]

This kind of instruction which asks and assumes so much is difficult to carry out. As we see in the stories, the approach suggested by Emerson and Bronson Alcott and portrayed by Louisa May Alcott addresses the individual rather than institutions. Again Louisa uses Emerson's and her father's approaches —love, sympathy, nourishment of the imagination, positive reinforcement, the withholding of approval, and the development of the conscience as the major means of discipline.

We have already explored in chapter 2 the lessons of the moral code that are drawn from the experiences of the child. In Alcott's stories, nature also plays an important role in the education of children. As Alcott drew her educational principles primarily from her father and Emerson, she drew her love and appreciation of nature as teacher primarily from Thoreau. The biographer Madelon Bedell writes of Thoreau's friendship with the Alcotts during his years at Walden Pond. "Always a person who communicated more easily with children than with adults, he became fast friends with the Alcott girls," she writes, "taking them on walks, picnics and boat rides at Walden Pond."[24] No child who had been on those expeditions could forget his vivid descriptions of the flowers and his lovely and clear playing of the flute.

Louisa never forgot. In her fiction, nature possesses remarkable remedial and recuperative powers, as several stories from the *Scrap-Bag* illustrate. In "Morning-Glories" (VI, 78-103), Aunt Laura, nicknamed Wee, teaches her niece Daisy to love learning. Both are standing on a mountaintop, where they have climbed on the last of their morning outings, viewing a powerful waterfall that turns the wheels of various mills. Aunt Laura had taught Daisy some valuable lessons, and Daisy is receptive to what she has to say. Aunt Laura tells Daisy that a giant more powerful than either stream or electricity lives in "that big house with the bell on the roof." She explains to Daisy the value of education:

> Education is a long word, dear; but you know what it means, and, as you grow older, you will see what wonders it can work. It is a noble giant; for in this country rich and poor are helped by it, and no one need suffer for it unless they choose. It works more wonders than any other: it changes little children into wise, good men and women, who rule the world, and make happy homes everywhere; it helps write books, sing songs, paint pictures, do good deeds, and beautify the world. Love and respect it, my little Daisy, and be glad that you live now when such giants lend a hand to dwarfs like us. (VI, 100-101)

Like the capable maiden aunts discussed in chapter 4, Aunt Laura has been called as a last resort to try to handle lazy, fretful, sickly Daisy. Aunt Laura's solution is a daily early-morning commune with nature: "A happy healthful hour in the morning sweetens and brightens the whole day; and there is no fairy-book so wonderful as the lovely world all about us, if we only know how to read it" (102). During these outings they visit

special places in the surrounding neighborhood, and Daisy has
a firsthand opportunity to learn of spiders and birds. Her interest revitalizes Daisy, and her parents are amazed at the change,
"for, though Daisy's frock was soiled, her boots wet, and her
hair tumbled, her cheeks were rosy, eyes bright, and voice so
cheerful that they thought it better music than any in the summer world without" (87).

Many of the children in the *Scrap-Bag* stories learn from nature by loving and caring for animals, an experience they can
cherish in spite of their poverty. A little like Bertie in "Little
Neighbors," Alcott says, "The language of animals I understand
without any grammar or dictionary" (III, 43). Two pieces in
the *Scrap-Bag* are narrative descriptions of favorite pets. In
"Huckleberry" (III, 41-53), she remembers the adopted stray
fondly: "Dear thing! how dirty, lean, and ugly he was! with
one lame foot, a torn ear, and a bit of old rope round his neck
where the collar should have been. Never mind; I loved him,
and went on petting him with a reckless disregard of consequences and fleas" (47). Another sketch, "Seven Black Cats"
(V, 52-66), describes a motely collection that "came uninvited"
to the Alcott house and died "tragical deaths." The animals
take on nearly human qualities, reflected in their names—Czar,
Blot, Mother Bunch, Imp, and so on. Knowing that most children love animals, she writes often of them, suggesting classic
themes that later authors develop. For example, in one story
a child befriends a mistreated animal. In "Old Major" (IV,
87-100) Ned saves an old horse from slaughter and allows him
to spend the last years at the same stable. The owner/narrator
relents and writes Rosa's story to pay the stable fee.

In these stories Alcott capitalizes on a long tradition of animal stories that goes back in Western culture at least to Aesop's
fables and anticipates a subgenre of children's stories that develops in the late nineteenth and continues into the twentieth
century—the animal story that tells of either the great friendship between a child and his or her pet or the story of an animal's life from the point of view of the animal. Both "Old
Major" and "Rosa's Tale" suggest some of the poignant scenes
that authors such as Anna Sewall was to capture in *Black Beauty* or Fred Gipson was to bring to life in *Old Yeller*.

The enjoyment of nature can be a solitary experience or one to be shared with a few friends. It requires little money, and no pretensions, simple comfortable clothes. In "What the Girls Did" (IV, 105-115), Nelly, whose father has recently lost a great deal of his fortune in a fire, is invited by a friend, Kitty, to a beach vacation spot for a lovely, yet simple, holiday. There is no necessity for an extravagant wardrobe; flannel boating suits suffice. There is plenty of swimming, hiking, and boating instead of dressing by day and dancing in hot rooms at night. The girls conclude the vacation joyously, attributing it to the magic of "old clothes, wholesome pleasures and charitable deeds." The vacation is exhilarating yet inexpensive, something that everyone can enjoy.

Although Alcott never takes the subject of appropriate dress for children, especially girls, as the major theme for a story, she addresses the subject whenever she can work it in, as she does in "What the Girls Did." She is incessant in arguing for comfortable clothes for girls that will permit them to breathe freely and move about unhampered, allowing them to exercise freely. Ultimately, it is her interest in nature that dictates this belief. The young woman who is limited by stays, laces, and high narrow heels simply has no freedom to explore what is about her—to run over the meadows, jump brooks, and climb trees and hills.

Closely related to the subject of dress are two other concerns that Alcott mentions again and again—the necessity of exercise and proper nutrition. Part of the recuperative power of the country is the fresh air, but the country also is ideal for walks and hikes that provide exercise while teaching of nature. Daisy blossoms from Aunt Laura's outings in "Morning-Glories"; the young seamstress Mary who joins the girls at the sea in "What the Girls Did" is rejuvenated; Jimmy's sister in "Jimmy's Cruise in the Pinafore" recovers during her outing in the country; and so on.

Perhaps influenced by her father's constant interest in health concerns, Alcott takes on the related subject of nutrition in "Lunch" (V, 89-104). In that story two spinsters decide that they must teach the young schoolboys of the neighborhood the relationship of good health to thinking skills—that "what

goes into children's stomachs affects their brains" (98). They
take up this responsibility after being appalled at the poor
quality of the food being sold to the boys by the neighborhood
baker. The women give up their patchwork and begin preparing
lunches for the boys. Much interest and a lighthearted tone is
created by the old women being nearly overwhelmed by the
vigorous antics of the young boys. But eventually they teach
them an important lesson. As Miss Hetty says, "Good, plain
victuals and plenty of 'em is the secret of firm health" (98).

The education and care of children that Alcott advocates in
her *Scrap-Bag* stories are designed to help them realize their potential. To read the stories is to observe a fictional portrayal of
what was later to be called progressive education and progressive parenting. The basic themes are similar: use of the direct
experiences of the child, direct participation in educational ven-
tures, and respect for the wisdom and intelligence of the child.
These beliefs, originally stated by her father and preached by
Emerson and the other transcendentalists, were popularized by
Alcott.

One has the feeling that, like the eagle who tells Alcott, "I
am a gentleman; therefore, I know how to behave," these children instinctively know what is best for them. The parents in
these stories guide their children by setting good examples, and,
when the parents and adults fail or lose sight of the right way,
the children redeem them.

Certainly Alcott's stories were a factor in shaping the change
that occurred in the nineteenth-century perception of children
from redeemable to redeemer. The stories appeared in periodicals read by hundreds of thousands of people. On the whole
they are consistent with the perceptions that the editors of
those magazines wished to encourage. The children in the stories are remarkably perceptive, precocious, intelligent, sensitive,
and mature. If there is a drawback or difficulty with these characterizations of children, perhaps it is that they are too good to
be true. If the story of the potentially perfect child loses interest, it may be that the example is too difficult to live up to.

If that is so, the form may have been altered to a less intense
story with a less intense moral theme—the adventure stories of
what Jane S. Smith calls "plucky little ladies and stout-hearted

chums."[25] These heroes and heroines of the serial novels that emerged at the turn of the century are credible because, through the work of earlier authors like Alcott, the readers came to believe that children can accomplish anything, leading readers to accept readily independent heroines who explore and solve mysteries, for example. These young girls can solve serious problems and escape precarious situations without the traditional protection of older brothers and fathers. The next chapter explores Alcott's treatment of the female role and suggests, in another way, how she set the stage for a more independent woman.

NOTES

1. Bronson Alcott, *Observations on the Life of My First Child (Anna Bronson Alcott) During Her First Year*, p. 27, quoted in Charles Strickland, "A Transcendentalist Father," *History of Childhood Quarterly*, I (Summer 1973), 4-51.
2. Bronson Alcott, quoted in Strickland, "A Transcendentalist Father," p. 12.
3. Ibid.
4. Whether Bronson succeeded too well in developing Louisa's sense of conscience is a question that interests all students of her writing. The biographer Martha Saxton has suggested that he did, and that Louisa's guilty devotion to her father thwarted her intellectual and artistic growth. See the final chapter of *Louisa May* (New York: Avon Books, 1977).
5. Niki Alpert McCurry, "Concepts of Childrearing and Schooling in the March Novels of Louisa May Alcott," Ph.D. Dissertation, Northwestern University, 1976. This dissertation analyzes "the March novels in the light of their author's own life and the life and educational practices of her father" (p. 3).
6. Peter Gregg Slater, *Children in the New England Mind* (Hamden, Conn.: Archon Books, 1977), p. 151. Slater calls Child's formulation of a theory of domestic education based on the notion of children as "little cherubs" a revolutionary act.
7. [Lydia Marie] Child, *The Mother's Book* (New York: Arno Press and the New York Times, 1972), p. 3.
8. Bruce Allen Ronda, "The Transcendental Child," Ph.D. Dissertation, Yale University, 1975, p. 12.
9. Ralph Waldo Emerson, "Education," *The Portable Emerson*, ed. Mark Van Doren (New York: The Viking Press, 1959), p. 257. Although

"Education" was not published until after Emerson's death in 1882, it was put together from pieces of his writing and can be considered representative of his thoughts on education and children. As editor Van Doren says, no subject ever interested Emerson more.

10. Bronson Alcott, quoted in Ronda, "The Transcendental Child," p. 126.

11. Ronda, "The Transcendental Child," p. 123.

12. Elizabeth Palmer Peabody, *Record of a School*, (New York: Arno Press and the New York Times, 1969), p. 132.

13. Ibid., p. 155.

14. Alma J. Payne, *Louisa May Alcott* (Boston: G. K. Hall & Co., 1980), p. 17.

15. Anne Tropp Trensky, "The Saintly Child in Nineteenth-Century American Fiction," *Prospects*, I (1975), 392.

16. Ednah D. Cheney, ed. *Louisa May Alcott* (Boston: Roberts Brothers, 1890), p. 270.

17. Leslie A. Fiedler, "Good Good Girls and Good Bad Boys," *Love and Death in the American Novel*, (New York: Stein and Day, 1975), pp. 259-290. Anne Tropp Trensky has also discussed the role of the naughty boy in "The Bad Boy in Nineteenth-Century American Fiction," *The Georgia Review*, 27 (Winter 1973), 503-517.

18. Madeleine B. Stern, *Louisa May Alcott* (Norman: University of Oklahoma Press, 1950), p. 70.

19. Alcott, *Plots and Counterplots* (New York: Popular Library, 1976), pp. 317-318.

20. Emerson, "Education," p. 255.

21. Ibid., p. 256.

22. Ibid., p. 254.

23. Ibid., p. 260.

24. Madelon Bedell, *The Alcotts* (New York: Clarkson N. Potter, Inc., 1980), p. 266.

25. Jane S. Smith, "Plucky Little Ladies and Stout-Hearted Chums," *Prospects*, 3 (1977), 155-174.

4

Women's Roles and "The Approaching Crisis in Women's Destiny"

Louisa May Alcott was reared among nineteenth-century New England's most intellectual women. Her mother, Abby, supported her father's devotion to truth and principle, even if she didn't always believe in his philosophical theories and practices. Though not formally educated, she read and wrote voluminously. She participated in the philosophical "conversations" that Bronson frequently held in their home. Lydia Marie Child was a friend of the Alcotts and visited the home occasionally. Elizabeth Peabody, classical scholar and pioneering educator, lived with the Alcotts for a time when she assisted Bronson at the Temple School, and Margaret Fuller visited Bronson at the Temple School and engaged in philosophical debate on educational and transcendental issues.

Louisa grew up hearing the most intellectual women of the age engage in heated discussions on women's changing roles. Her father's radical educational notions included support for education for women as well as men. Her mother also supported her intellectual development. She bought Louisa a desk for Christmas 1852, saying to her husband, "She is a fine bright girl [who] only needs encouragement to be a brave woman. . . . I am inclined to think the approaching crisis in women's destiny will find a place of no mean magnitude for her."[1]

The role Louisa chose for herself was atypical but acceptable. Since the beginning of the nineteenth century, women had been writing stories and novels for women and children and child-rearing advice manuals for parents. Often they turned to this

profession out of financial necessity, as Louisa did. The work
was acceptable and convenient because it could be done within
the confines of the "woman's sphere," during the time women
were not engaged in domestic tasks. Because of Bronson's un-
willingness to support the family through traditional salaried
jobs, Louisa and her mother were forced to enter the labor market. Louisa had seen Abby take in sewing, do social work for
the poor of Boston, and run an employment agency for Boston
women. Louisa herself had taught, taken in sewing, and worked
as a domestic.

Although Louisa always felt responsible for the usual domestic tasks, she never relegated herself solely to that responsibility.
Neither had her mother, nor the many women within Alcott's
circle of friends and acquaintances. Certainly Abby never
wanted for her daughters the usual resolution of marriage to a
rich man. As we have said before, Louisa realized that she "was
married to" her writing. There is a sense of worldliness in her
life's activities that reveals a sensitivity to and sympathy with
the broader educational and social issues of the day involved
in "the approaching crisis in women's destiny." Although the
phrase is originally her mother's, Louisa adopts variations on
it in several of her stories. She never explicitly defines the "approaching crisis," but evidence in the *Scrap-Bag* stories suggests
that the crisis has to do with the suffrage issue and the promise
for change in women's status that the vote would bring. The
changes would permit women greater access to higher education and thus allow them to prepare for professional careers
and to assume positions of public responsibility. Alcott's journals show that she was always interested in the question of
women's suffrage and worked to support it, as her mother had.
This chapter examines the roles for women that Alcott portrays in her *Scrap-Bag* stories and considers how these roles are
consistent with and yet suggest departures from those typically
prescribed for nineteenth-century women.

Alcott's women are not ardent feminists at the forefront of
the women's movement, but they are aware that an important
change is occurring, and they are preparing for it. Their preparation is education, so that they might understand the consequences of their new duties. In the meantime, they continue

to fulfill their old duties well. They believe that the greatest opportunities fall within the family and social relationships, and they work within the system to improve it.

Now and then there is within her writing a glimpse of another role that is less traditional. It is suggested in small ways: in the tempestuous freewheeling personality of Jo in *Little Women*, in the insistence of women in several of the novels that they must establish independence before they marry, and in the personal beliefs that Alcott suggests in the nonfiction narratives. These less traditional themes are explored and an attempt is made to place them in perspective later in the chapter. But, first, to the traditional models in the *Scrap-Bags*.

"FITTING OURSELVES FOR NEW DUTIES BY DOING OLD ONES WELL"

The story that discusses "the approaching crisis in women's destiny" most explicitly is the title story of Volume III of the *Scrap-Bag*, "Cupid and Chow-Chow" (III, 1-40), the longest story in the collection. Because it spells out very clearly the position that Alcott takes in her short stories, it is worth looking at in some detail.

The story is an explanation of the changing relationship between a young boy, Cupid, and his cousin, Chow-Chow,[2] and the insights that their parents gain from observing their antics. In fact, the lesson of the story seems directed to parents as well as children, a common practice among children's writers. The message includes a knowledge of social and cultural affairs and subtleties that are beyond a child's understanding, yet the story is told in such a way that there are levels of appreciation for both children and adults, much as the classic novel *The Adventures of Huckleberry Finn* can be read successfully on both levels.

Cupid and Chow-Chow are among the most interesting children in the stories, partly because they are among the most unusual. Their extreme characterizations reverse the stereotypical portrayals of little boys and girls, allowing Alcott to develop obvious points about appropriate roles. Cupid, a Good Good boy, is a handsome, effeminate child who is dressed in velvets

7. "Don't be frightened. I'm Cupid. I must kiss you. I truly must."
    Cupid and Chow-Chow, Etc., Vol. 3.

8. The wounded hero, with his arm in a sling, permitted her to minister to him. *Cupid and Chow-Chow, Etc.*, Vol. 3.

and satins and pampered by his mother. Although he is loving
and considerate, the excessive attention of his mother has
caused him to become vain and spoiled. Alcott describes him
thus:

> Especially beautiful and attractive did he look as he
> pranced on the doorsteps one afternoon while waiting
> the arrival of a little cousin. Our Cupid's costume was
> modernized out of regard to the prejudices of society,
> and instead of wings, bandage, bow and arrow, he was
> gorgeous to behold in small buckled shoes, purple silk
> hose, black velvet knickerbockers, and jacket with a lace
> collar, which, with his yellow hair cut straight across the
> forehead, and falling in long, curling love-locks behind,
> made him look like an old picture of a young cavalier. (2)

The conflict emerges when young Cousin Chow-Chow and
her parents arrive for a prolonged visit. Chow-Chow, in contrast to Cupid, is a Good Bad girl, "a little figure, dressed in a
brown linen frock, with dusty boots below it, and above it a
head of wild black hair, tied up with a large scarlet bow, [who]
stood by the pond throwing stones at the swans, who ruffled
their feathers in stately anger at such treatment" (15).

The two other important characters in the story are their
mothers, Ellen and Susan, whom Alcott holds responsible for
their children's behavior. The fathers are colorless—less strong-
willed than their wives and willing to go along with the events,
pace, and tone that the women suggest. The conflict begins
when Cupid welcomes Chow-Chow with a kiss, and Chow-
Chow responds by pushing him away and throwing a handful
of gravel in his face. Chow-Chow's father rationalizes her behavior:

> "And I predict a hard time of it for your young man,
> if he attempts to tame my strong-minded little woman
> here. Her mother's ideas are peculiar, and she wants to
> bring Chow-Chow up according to the new lights,—with
> contempt for dress and all frivolous pursuits, to make her
> hardy, independent, and quite above caring for such

trifles as love, domestic life, or the feminine accomplish-
ments we used to find so charming." (7)

Susan, Chow-Chow's mother, a worker in the women's suffrage movement, has qualities similar to her daughter—a plain
dress, an unbecoming hair style, and a "decided mouth, sarcas-
tic nose, and restless eyes that seemed always on the watch to
find some new wrong and protest against it" (8). In contrast,
Ellen, Cupid's mother, is portrayed as reasonable and suppor-
tive. When asked by Susan why she doesn't prepare Cupid "to
take a nobler part in the coming struggle [with women's suf-
frage] than those who have come before," Ellen replies, "I
don't care to disturb his happy childhood with quarrels beyond
his comprehension. I shall teach him to be as good and just a
man as his father, and feel quite sure that no woman will suffer wrong at his hands" (9-10).
As the days progress, Chow-Chow "rides rough-shod" over
Cupid, taunting him for his long curls, vain manners, and "girl-
boy" ways, teasing him into allowing her to cut his hair, manipulating him into proving his courage by putting his finger into
the cogs of wheels of a hay-cutting machine. Yet when Cupid's
hand is seriously injured, Chow-Chow is compassionate. Her
father says, "I have hopes of her yet, for all the woman is not
taken out of her, in spite of the new lights" (16). Cupid's courage during the recovery process shows her "the difference between the rash daring that runs foolish risks, and the steady
courage that bears pain without complaint" (18). Chow-Chow's
mother, Susan, perceives the situation as "a good lesson in sur-
gery and nursing" for her daughter, whom she hopes will study
medicine. But Ellen hopes that it will be "a good lesson in loving and serving others for love's sake, as all women must learn
to do soon or late" (20).
Chow-Chow soon reverts to her previous harsh behavior, and
Ellen's attempts to "soften" her and teach her "sundry feminine arts" are unsuccessful. Finally, however, Chow-Chow
learns her lesson during an extended scene of "playing house"
in which the children role-play the normal sequence of their
parents' day, a foil which allows Alcott to discuss adult roles
and relationships in the guise of children's play.

Through the events of the game, Chow-Chow realizes that she is lonely and selfish. Her mother, who has been observing with the other parents, acknowledges her daughter's miserable behavior: "I was going on to say that, finding she has done wrong, I hope she will have the courage to say so, hard as it is, and to expiate her fault and try to do better" (33). But Chow-Chow doesn't relent so easily. She insists on pretending that she is lecturing at a woman's suffrage meeting. When Susan confesses the absurdity of her daughter's play, Ellen reassures her, "There is some sense in it, and I have no doubt the real and true will come to pass when we women learn how far to go, and how to fit ourselves for the new duties by doing the old ones well" (34). She continues:

> She is like so many of those who mount your hobby, Susan, and ride away into confusions of all sorts, leaving empty homes behind them. The happy, womanly women will have the most influence after all, and do the most to help the bitter, sour, discontent ones. They need help, God knows, and I shall be glad to lend a hand toward giving them their rights in all things. (35)

As Chow-Chow mounts the platform at her imaginary "suffrage meeting," she falls, to be rescued from serious injury by Cupid. But she gains insight from her close call and declares, "I'll never play that nasty old puckerage any more" (36). Her father reminds Chow-Chow—the reminder is intended for her mother, Susan, as well—to examine her beliefs and commitments in the future: "Be sure that your platform is all right before you try again, else it will let you down when you least expect it, and damage your best friends as well as yourself" (36).

Alcott applauds Chow-Chow's change of heart, saying, "like a true woman, though she demanded impossibilities at first, yet when her heart was won she asked nothing but love, and was content with a saucepan" (38). The children resolve their difficulties by vowing that "the fairest way is to cut it 'zactly in halves, . . . that's the right thing to do always" (39). Alcott concludes the story with a reminder that the parents (especially Chow-Chow's mother) have learned a lesson from the children, thus assuring "that the future would be happier than the past" (40).

This story, with its message directed at both parents and children, suggests the practical position that Alcott adopts in all of her stories. It is a position born of the belief that the best way to correct a situation or to prepare for change is to work within the traditional institutions. The stories suggest again and again that those in control will be reponsive to those who wish change and need support, as Ellen assumes her husband will respond reasonably, if the requests are sensibly and intelligently made. There is a realization that the change will be gradual, but this offers the comfort of having time to prepare for the opportunities that will come. A broad education that begins in the early years with faithful instruction from the mother is the best preparation.

DOMESTIC FEMINISM AND "THE APPROACHING CRISIS IN WOMEN'S DESTINY"

"To fit ourselves for the new duties by doing the old ones well." What a wealth of meaning in a single assertion! It acknowledges what both Louisa and her mother call "the approaching crisis in women's destiny"; it suggests a cautious approval and acceptance of change; it assumes for women significant roles; it implies an intelligent, questioning preparation for those roles; yet it affirms the traditional roles and values of the "woman's sphere." Things are to be cut " 'zactly in halves," with women assuming responsibility for the domestic half.

Embodied in the assertion is a contradiction that is puzzling to twentieth-century feminists who have been critical of the stance. There is an acknowledgment and approval of coming changes, yet a definition of women's responsibilities in such a way as to keep them from moving out of traditional roles, thus making change difficult. It appears to place women in stasis, acknowledging change yet not being able to alter traditional roles to bring it about. Those who criticize this stance might say that Susan is betraying both her cause and herself when she gives up her suffrage meetings, or they might charge that the portrait of the activists, because of its extreme characterization, is unfair.

Sandra M. Gilbert and Susan Gubar have taken a radical feminist point of view in their recent study of nineteenth-century female writers.[3] They attribute the failure of many female authors to achieve greatness as due to the fact that they were nurtured in the patriarchal literary tradition and therefore anxious about assuming a public literary role. They suggest that Alcott moved from the strong artistic work of *Little Women* to "moral homilies for children" because she could not move out of the patriarchal framework. She also failed to develop the potential of her gothic thrillers. They suggest that "there is conscious or semiconscious irony in all the choices of the miniature over the assuredly major, of the domestic over the dramatic, of the private over the public, of obscurity over glory." And they conclude that Alcott's need "to make such choices emphasizes the sickening anxiety of authorship inherent in the situation of almost every woman writer in England and America until quite recently."[4]

But it seems that they deliver this devastating critique by assessing the fiction from a traditional point of view that ascribes more importance to tales of adventure and the sea, for example, than to those of hearth and home. The domestic drama has been assigned a pejorative connotation that the female writers of the nineteenth century either did not perceive or chose to ignore, assuming its fault because it overlooked a major subject of richness that the domestic arena offered. The definition of what is major or what is public or what is full of glory is, after all, subject to one's point of view. And, as suggested in the introduction, these women suffered little anxiety but chose instead to operate as professional writers rather than literary artists.

As they wrote, they worked from the sphere of domesticity that has been described beautifully by Nancy F. Cott in *The Bonds of Womanhood.* She has shown how the idea of the woman's sphere emerged early in the nineteenth century with the increasingly widening gap between women's work and men's work and how that development caused women's work to seem less systematized and urgent than men's because it eluded ra-

tionalization and the cash nexus and integrated labor with life.
Yet, as Cott points out, the canon of domesticity, in separating
the women's sphere from the men's, gave women a sense of satisfaction as well as solidarity. And female education, which encouraged women to understand gender as the essential deter-
miner of their lives, gave women a sense that they shared a
common destiny. It is only another step, she suggests, to sense
that they might shape that destiny. Her study concludes with
the notion that the women's sphere opened the opportunities
of domestic influence, religious morality, and child nurture.
It also articulated social power based on female qualities rather
than general human rights—a necessary stage in shattering the
hierarchy of sex and softening the hierarchical relationship of
marriage.

Within the last few years, women's social history scholars
have suggested that women sought change in the traditional
roles by working within the system. They point out that this
is a valid approach and that the women who worked within
this system held basically the same insistence on equal political, economic, and social rights as the public feminists. Those
who chose to work within the system for these rights (as Aunt
Ellen does in "Cupid and Chow-Chow") were domestic feminists.

The term domestic feminism was adopted by Daniel Scott
Smith in "Family Limitation, Sexual Control and Domestic
Feminism in Victorian America," in which he argues that by
exerting their autonomy through sexual control, women were
successful in limiting family size. Scott defines domestic feminism as "the extension of autonomy of women within the
family and the gradual enlargement of the social territory assigned to the domestic sphere."[5] Smith explains the emergence
of domestic feminism as a "nineteenth-century creation, born
out of the emerging conjugal family and the social stresses ac-
companying modern economic growth." He continues:

> Instead of postulating woman as an atom in competitive
> society, domestic feminism viewed woman as a person in
> the context of relationships with others. By defining the
> family as a community, this ideology allowed women to

engage in something of a critique of male, materialistic, market society and simultaneously proceed to seize power within the family. Women asserted themselves within the family much as their husbands were attempting to assert themselves outside the home.[6]

Smith claims domestic feminism was the only opening within the system. Judging from the short stories she published in the periodicals of the day, apparently Alcott did too. (I will suggest later how her personal beliefs may have differed from the themes she presented in her stories.) In assuming this stance, she was following a tradition of earlier female novelists of the nineteenth century whose writing represents a "moderate, or limited, or pragmatic feminism" that was "constrained by certain other types of beliefs that are less operative today." In her study of such authors, Nina Baym suggests that for these women experience was defined by "models of interpersonal relationships rather than classes, castes or other institutional structures."[7] In other words, human interactions counted far more than membership in various social or economic groups.

Both Smith and Baym point to the importance of personal relationships. Smith says that women seized the opportunity to work within the "community" of the family to effect change, and Baym points out that, when these female novelists composed, they chose the community of the family and other personal relationships as the subject of their novels. Their protagonists' assertion of themselves in the course of the novels represents "unspectacular feminism." The basic story line of many of the female novelists shows a woman who starts out as unwilling and incapable of fending for herself. In the course of the novels, often because circumstances force her to, she changes her perception of herself and develops "a strong conviction of her own worth."

The genre of the short story prohibits Alcott from portraying the change that the characters in the longer fiction undergo. Alcott's technique is to present models of various sorts of women engaged in conflicts that teach children (both in her stories and audience), models to imitate and reject. In this way, once again, her didactic approach is similar to other nineteenth-century female authors who insist that their heroines take responsibility for their difficulties, even if not of their own making, and overcome them.

This decision to assume responsibility is an example from Alcott's fiction of what Nancy Cott calls a necessary stage in the movement of women toward equality. Just as the female novelists assumed that the readers would accept the author's solution to difficulties as pertinent to their own lives, so Alcott assumed that the young reader would identify with, and hence internalize, the same lesson that the young children in the story learned. Before exploring some of the ways in which Alcott teaches these lessons, let us examine a social role that she encourages her readers to reject—that of the "social butterfly."

THE OBJECTION TO "SOCIAL BUTTERFLIES"

Alcott is very clear throughout all her fiction that she has little respect for those women who make no positive contributions to society. In January 1868 she wrote an advice column called "Happy Women" for the *New York Ledger*, which included "sketches of single women, doctors, teachers, and writers who made their lives models of purpose, self-denial, usefulness, and cheer."[8] The idea of such women as models is apparent in several stories of the fourth volume of the *Scrap-Bag*.

In a personal narrative called "My Girls," the title story of Volume IV of the *Scrap-Bag*, Alcott describes six "girls" who are models of "purpose, self-denial, usefulness, and cheer." In a justification that seems typical of mid-twentieth-century non-sexist language concerns, Alcott defends her use of the term: "Several of them are girls no longer; but as they are still unmarried, I like to call them by their old name, because they are so young at heart, and have so beautifully fulfilled the promise of their youth, not only by doing, but being excellent and admirable women" (5).

To qualify as "excellent and admirable," each woman must have a noble goal. Alcott explains that initially she had dismissed all who were well-to-do. "Poor girls," she writes, "always had my sympathy and respect, for necessity soon makes brave women of them if they have any strength or talent in them; but the well-to-do girls usually seemed to me like pretty

butterflies, leading easy, aimless lives when the world was full
of work which ought to be done" (7-8). Eventually she realizes
that not all wealthy girls "belong to the 'butterfly species' "
and discovers some who have "won the battle"—read law,
studied medicine, devoted themselves to music, and gave time,
money, and heart to charity.

In another story in the same volume, "Autobiography of an
Omnibus" (IV, 187-204), Alcott attacks social butterflies by
comparing them with simpler girls. The omnibus, which is telling its life story, remembers:

> The young girls . . . then . . . [were] so simply dressed, so
> quiet in manner, so unconscious of display, and so full of
> innocent gayety, that the crustiest passenger could not
> help softening as they came in. Bless their dear hearts!
> What would they say if they could see the little fashion-
> plates . . . now? The seven-story hats with jet daggers,
> steel arrows, and gilt horse-shoes on the sides, peacocks'
> tails in front, and quantities of impossible flowers tum-
> bling off behind. The jewelry, the frills and bows, the
> frizzled hair and high-heeled boots, and, worst of all, the
> pale faces, tired eyes, and ungirlish manners.
>   . . . They are only what the times make them,—fast and
> loud, frivolous and feeble. (189-190)

In "Red Tulips" (IV, 205-217), Helen discovers "that life
was not all a summer day, and she was something better than
a butterfly." Her friends discover that Helen "had improved
. . . wonderfully, for behind the belle, they found a tender-
hearted woman" (213). And, most important for Helen, her
conversion wins the heart of Dr. Strong, who had previously
rejected her because of her frivolous ways. "I was mistaken,
and judged too hastily last year," he says to himself. "Helen
is not what I thought her, a frivolous, fashionable beauty, but
a sweet, sensible girl, who is tired of that empty life, and quietly tries to make it beautiful and useful in the best and truest
way" (215).

Alcott's objection to the frivolous belle is that all the efforts
she must expend on her social life and appearance keep her

9. "The Autobiography of an Omnibus," *My Girls, Etc.,* Vol. 4.

from fulfilling her obligation to her family and to herself. For instance, in "The Moss People" (III, 157-181), a little girl named Marnie teaches her mother to "attend more to the comfort of home, and not care so much for fashionable society." Little Marnie intuits the message with which she must reform her mother through the contrivance of a dream. As Alcott often does when she attacks sensitive issues, she uses dream/fantasy creatures to tell her story.

Marnie falls asleep on a rainy day and dreams of a fantasy land inhabited by moss people pretending they are humans. Their routine satirizes social customs:

> "Lace me tightly. I'm growing stout . . . and my figure will be ruined if I allow it," said madam; and Dimity squeezed her into such a tight dress that Trip got a pain in her side directly. "I can bear it a little while, but I don't see how ladies can do it all the time,—it's dreadful!" she sighed, as Dimity piled her pretty hair in a fuzzy bunch on the top of her head, and hung jewels in her little ears, after putting costly bits of lace here and there, and poking her tiny feet into high-heeled boots that made her totter when she tried to walk. (167)

Next, Alcott deplores the custom of "calling." The women gossip only of clothes, servants, and men. After one leaves, the remaining women talk behind her back. And when they all depart, the hostess says, "Tiresome, ill-natured creatures, I can't bear any of them; but I must return their calls as soon as my new bonnet comes from Paris" (168). Dinner brings unexpected, officious guests who consume too much ill-prepared food. Then the husband goes off for a ride with his guests (without his wife, who must prepare for an evening party). After tea comes the party, and Alcott relentlessly continues:

> Such dashing little beaux and belles as did arrive, dressed in the most astonishing style,—the ladies with bits of bouquets and fans, satin slippers, and trailing skirts. The gentlemen had stiff collars, gay ties, wee boots and gloves, and twirled their eye-glasses as if they

> had been going to parties all their lives. Every one sim-
> pered and chatted, laughed and flirted, looked at each
> other's clothes, and whispered gossip round the room.
> (176)

Dancing follows supper, and the guests leave, complimenting
their hosts while still inside the house and being snidely critical
as soon as they leave: " 'Wasn't it a miserable affair? Those
Prances are very ordinary people, and I shall not go again' "
(177).

When Marnie confides her dream to her mother, she immediately sees the point and vows to spend less time with "fashionable society." The parties consume time and energy, the clothes
are uncomfortable, the conversation trivial, the friendships superficial, and the food unpalatable and unnutritious. And, in
the meantime, the relationships that count suffer. There is constant tension between the husband and wife for failing to meet
one anothers' unreasonable demands, and they both neglect
their children in their desire to fulfill their social obligations.

Being a social butterfly engages one's time and energy in such
a way that it keeps one from attending to "noble" things. These
women are not taking themselves seriously. At the beginning of
Rose in Bloom, Rose tells her Uncle Alec, "I know it is foolish;
but I do want to be a regular butterfly for a little while and see
what it is like."[9] After three months, she realizes the futility of
the social whirl. She understands that "her fortune is her chief
attraction" and that her friends, like those of Mrs. Prance in
"The Moss People," are superficial. She resolves, "I'm going to
set about living in earnest," and she finds all sorts of charitable
and family works to do. By the conclusion of the novel, she
has discovered a new identity, which Alcott summarizes by
having Rose quote Emerson's advice to women in "Self-Reliance": " 'Let the maiden, with erect soul, walk serenely on her
way; accept the hint of each new experience; search in turn all
the objects that solicit her eye, that she may learn the power
and the charm of her newborn being.' "[10]

Meg's flirtation with the social whirl in *Little Women* is as
unsatisfactory as Rose's. Although initially impressed by Meg's
good looks and pleasant charm, Meg's friends eventually ridi-

cule her worn, dated dress and gossip about her poverty. When Meg returns from the ball, she confesses to her mother that she had initially been captivated by the glamour and excitement but that she had seen the superficiality of it all. Marmee consoles her: "Don't be troubled, Meg, . . . make this home happy so that you may be fit for homes of your own, if they are offered you, and contented here if they are not."[11] Marmee concludes this moral lesson with a variation on Miss Ellen's theme from "Cupid and Chow-Chow":

> My dear girls, I *am* ambitious for you, but not to have you make a dash in the world—marry rich men merely because they are rich, or have splendid houses, which are not homes because love is wanting. Money is a needful and precious thing—and, when well used, a noble thing— but I never want you to think it is the first or only prize to strive for. I'd rather see you poor men's wives, if you were happy, beloved, contented, than queens on thrones, without self-respect and peace.[12]

Alcott suggests that women are drawn to the role of social butterfly because they feel they have nothing to offer if they don't present themselves in that role. Rose in *Rose in Bloom* expresses the fear this way: "I want to be or do something splendid. . . . I can't write poetry or sing like a bird; but I should think I might have my share of glory in some way. . . . Do you think I have *any* gift that could be cultivated?"[13] Her Uncle Alec responds that her gift is "the art of living for others . . . patiently and sweetly."

The corrective to being a social butterfly is for young women to take themselves seriously and to work within the sphere of personal relationships to do good—"the art of living for others." This dedication includes charitable and professional work, but family responsibilities assume first priority. Rose's friend Phebe decides to give up a promising career in opera ("fame and fortune and the admiration of many a . . . man") to devote herself to her husband. Phebe has established her independence, but feels that the rewards and opportunities will be greater for her within the framework of personal family relationships. In condemning social butterflies, Alcott follows the practice of earlier nineteenth-century female authors who deplore both the passive woman and her "apparent opposite," the belle.[14]

The prominence of labor as the first tenet of the moral code suggests that Alcott would have no patience with a passive woman; the girls and women in her stories act on their environment rather than allow themselves to be acted upon. The belle was a modern woman whose life was much like that of Mrs. Prance of "The Moss People," devoted to seeking the admiration of party-goers, with the mistaken notion that the attention she garnered for herself was equivalent to power and influence. Alcott's satirical treatment of such creatures in "The Moss People" makes it quite clear that she realized that such women were unwittingly aiding the money system that was at cross-purposes with their desire for fulfillment. The social whirl that Mrs. Prance realizes she must escape is costly—the maintenance of a lovely home, elaborately furnished, impeccably kept by a staff of servants within and gardeners without; the display of a fashionable wardrobe, resplendent with satins and jewels. Alcott certainly realized, as Baym argues that the other nineteenth-century female authors did, that "the rage for money was the greatest threat to the dignity of woman's life and to the moral life of the entire nation. The cult of domesticity is a social concept that replaces the marketplace with the home, and the belle has given herself to the marketplace."[15]

The fact that most nineteenth-century female authors attacked the belle is a point that Ann Douglas overlooks in *The Feminization of American Culture*, her recent study of the relationship between the clergy and the female writers of the day. She sees the choice for personal relationships and the "selling" of the woman to the marketplace as leading, ultimately, to an obsession with mediocrity for women. In her study, Douglas argues that the typical heroine was a woman whose beauty gave her invulnerability and who lost her practical role in the household merely to become a symbol of expenditure. Eventually, she suggests, women lost their ability to run households and save lives and become promulgators of influence. She uses

the example of Harriet Beecher Stowe's Eva van Ardsdel, heroine of *My Wife and I* and *We and Our Neighbors*, to help prove
her point.[16]

Yet it is important to remember that Stowe's work is an exception to the nineteenth-century female writers we have previously mentioned. Slavery and religion are subjects that assume
more importance for her than gender. Although some of the
women in Stowe's later fiction "sell" themselves to the marketplace, there are other women in Stowe's fiction who are called
upon because of their devotion to contemporary causes to engage in various acts of civil disobedience. They want education,
employment opportunities at fair wages, and eventual participation in the political process.[17]

Douglas believes, as she suggests in her chapter on Margaret
Fuller, that the only viable role for a woman in the nineteenth
century was essentially a revolutionary one. Her consistent
negative use of the word "domestic" suggests that she has failed
to assess these women on their own terms, as Nancy F. Cott
does successfully in her study of the woman's sphere. In failing
to do so, she failed to understand how women could see the
political opportunities of the vote, for instance, as less important
than the social and educational opportunities offered within the
framework of the home, the heart of all relationships.

Although Alcott criticizes the social butterfly, she doesn't
necessarily blame her, realizing that society expects women to
fulfill that role. The assignment of women to the domestic
sphere has relegated women to the home. In the case of the
social butterfly, her work there is merely displaying wealth
through elaborate and expensive dress and social rituals such
as the custom of "calling." Alcott's women find such "work"
exhausting and unrewarding, empty and devoid of meaning.
Instead, they choose "noble ends" that involve working for the
good of their families and others.

Alcott emphasizes the emptiness of a role that Thorstein
Veblen was to describe nearly thirty years later when he pointed out that it had become the "office of the women to consume
vicariously for the head of the household." He explained that it
had become improper for such respectable women to engage in
productive labor. The construction of their dress was to impress

others with the "fact (indeed, sometimes a fiction) that the wearer does not and cannot engage in useful work." He concludes that such a woman's sphere is "within the household, which she should 'beautify,' and of which she should be the 'chief ornament.' "[18]

Alcott believes that the social butterfly has been educated improperly. Her anti-intellectual role has trivialized her. As the mother in "The Moss People" laments, "I never was taught to do any thing but look pretty" (III, 195). The answer lies in a well-rounded education that includes practical skills as well as tough book-learning. Gwen, in "How They Camped Out" (V, 119-140), learns this lesson the hard way.

A group of eight children depart on a sleighing party. Because their coachman has been drinking, he allows the horses to run off after the group has been stranded at a lodge in a snowstorm. Gwen, the eldest, resourcefully takes charge. The children light a fire and snack on apples and nuts. But eventually, they get hungry again. Alcott sends the boys to the rescue. "Girls aren't worth much in the hour of need," says one of the boys. They forage, find some meal and jam, improvise a cooking arrangement, melt snow, mix batter, and bake cakes. Gwen is unable to help because she can't cook, although she was "unusually accomplished in French, German, and music." Gwen also fails through a lack of courage. Startled by the rescuers, whom she mistakes as intruders, she screams, and then faints. The story concludes with Gwen's resolution to "learn cooking and courage."

Gwen's resolution embodies the two major recommendation: Alcott makes to her young readers. One is to take themselves seriously, to face up to their responsibilities both to others and to themselves. They must realize that their acts can have a positive impact on the lives of their families and others. When this realization dawns, they will give up things of little consequence and devote themselves to "nobler" ends. What Alcott calls the devotion to nobler ends is similar to the goals of the protagonists of other nineteenth-century novels by women, who develop a strong conviction of their own worth, which leads them to set high goals for themselves and which changes both their perception of themselves and others' perceptions of them.

The nobler ends that are developed through this altered perception of self-worth are achieved through preparedness, which leads to Alcott's second recommendation—women need a well-rounded education. That education, which begins in the home with the mother's informal instruction, should include practical subjects as well as traditionally feminine and masculine ones. In emphasizing practical studies Alcott is following the tradition of Benjamin Franklin, who recommended that education for both men and women should serve utilitarian purposes; of Benjamin Rush, who argued in *Thoughts on Female Education* that women should be educated for social utility; and of numerous nineteenth-century women such as Sarah Hale and Elizabeth Peabody, who supported a well-rounded practical education for women. In arguing for study in such subjects as mathematics and science, Alcott was working against the tradition that held that knowledge of those subjects might rob women of their charms and lead them to neglect the practical.

WOMEN'S ROLES AND THE
AFFIRMATION OF THE FAMILY

At the heart of all happy families in Alcott's fiction is a mother, who is something of a saint. Even if Alcott portrays a family that is motherless, the memory of the mother sets the tone for the others. If life runs smoothly for the family members, it is probably because of the mother, who keeps it that way. She is described in "What Fanny Heard" (III, 181-189) as "happy, for duty was pleasant" and "bright . . . and never out of tune." Her "gentle ways, her loving heart, her cheerful voice, and willing hands" are described in more detail:

> She tended flowers in the window yonder, and grew as beautiful as they; she touched the old piano, and filled the house with music; she fed her little bird, and was as cheerful as he; she read and studied those books, growing wise and good and gay on the food they gave her; she sewed busily, clothing naked children as well as dolls, and many blessed her. She often lay where you lie now, not discontented and sad, but with a happy heart, a busy

fancy, and the love of many friends to keep her always blithe. (188)

Since Fanny's duty is to act like her mother, is it any wonder she is fussy, idle, and disobedient? The task seems nearly impossible. Yet this is the model that the young women in the stories are expected to imitate, and the memory of her mother convinces Fanny to try. She vows: "O dear mamma, I will be you, if I can: I'll find friends where you found them; I'll make home happy as you did. I'll try to be loved for your sake, and grow a useful, cheerful, good woman, like you" (189)

The portraits of mothers in Alcott's fiction are all very positive. The few exceptions fall into the "social butterfly" category discussed earlier. These women still love and care for their families; it is simply that their actions and energies are misguided. There is only one portrait of a wayward mother in the six volumes of the *Scrap-Bags*. Again, as Alcott does so often when dealing with controversial and touchy themes, she turns to the time-honored tradition of the fable to dramatize her story of maternal neglect. To show the serious, indeed fatal, consequences in inadequate mothering, Alcott creates "the unfortunate family of the Clucks." In "Madam Cluck, and Her Family" (I, 100-110), all eight chicks meet their fate because Madam Cluck "didn't know how to manage them" and because she failed to teach them proper virtues. Although a tragic story, it is told in a light tone. Chanty's boldness and pride leads to his death by a game cock; Downy and Snowball are careless and drown; Speckle, misled by Aunt Cockletop (the only aunt in the stories who gives bad advice), misapprehends danger and is killed by a hawk; Strut dies when trying to crow from the highest beam; Peep fails to learn moderation and eats herself to death in the mealbin; Peck is indiscriminate and dies of an overdose of salt; and the final member of the flock dies attempting to help a stray kitten. This intolerable maternal neglect is punished when Madam Cluck and the useless Aunt Cockletop are served up as a Thanksgiving feast.

In the *Scrap-Bag* stories the father plays a minor role. If present, as in "Cupid and Chow-Chow," they reflect the tone and go along with the example and pace their wives set. Such

is the case in *Little Women*. In one passage where Jo has been
working to reign in her temper, Marmee confides that she too
had had difficulty controlling her temper. She explains that
her mother and husband have helped her gain control: "I've
learned to check the hasty words that rise to my lips, and
when I feel that they mean to break out against my will, I just
go away a minute, and give myself a little shake for being so
weak and wicked."[19] She explains her husband's support:

> He helped and comforted me, and showed me that I must
> try to practice all the virtues I would have my little girls
> possess, for I was their example. It was easier to try for
> your sakes than for my own; a startled or surprised look
> from one of you when I spoke sharply rebuked me more
> than any words could have done; and the love, respect,
> and confidence of my children was the sweetest reward
> I could receive for my efforts to be the woman I would
> have them copy.[20]

Acknowledging her mother's saintliness, Jo cries, "If I'm ever
half as good as you, I shall be satisfied." Father March is away
at the war for nearly half of the novel. When he is present, he
remains in the background, acting as counselor and supporter,
while Marmee is the guiding light.

Mother is all things to all people: to her husband she is companion; to her children she is teacher as well as comforter; to
her community she is often resource person and informal social
worker. If her husband is absent or dead, she is provider, all
with a sense of cheerful grace, if not ease. Mother has accepted
responsibility for her role, and has respect for the power and
opportunity it affords her. In fact, her essence is so strong that,
should she die, her children can succeed without her, committed
to her memory. In this sense, all Alcott families are matriarchal.

In "Kate's Choice" (III, 128-157), Alcott explores "the tender reverence which is the beautiful tribute the young should
pay the old." In this case, orphan Kate comes to live with her
relatives in America. The conflict centers around her decision
of where to live. She can choose from among the families of her
four uncles, yet she is surprised at how they all ignore their

grandmother, excluding her from family activities—"how could they live without a grandmother?" Kate decides to visit the grandmother before making her decision. Not surprisingly, she eventually decides to stay with her permanently, but not before she brings the family to their senses and gently shames them for their rejection of their grandmother. In typical Alcott fashion, the story culminates at a Christmas holiday for which Kate has organized a family celebration. The love and warmth of the grandmother are able to work their magic. The family members regret and compensate for their years of neglect, and Grandma wins Kate, really the mother-figure in the story.

Volume IV of the *Scrap-Bag* concludes with "A Happy Birthday" (218-229), the narrative description of a birthday celebration of a seventy-three-year-old grandmother. The tale, which Louisa sold to *Youth's Companion* for fifty dollars, is based on the celebration of Louisa's mother's seventy-third birthday at Orchard House, in which all of the family members come to pay their homage.[21]

Throughout her short stories, as well as her novels, Alcott uses the rituals and festivities associated with holidays and birthdays as settings for her stories. The holidays and birthdays offer an excuse for joy and cheer, and Alcott capitalizes on these occasions to celebrate the family. In describing such a holiday, Alcott writes, "Some families do not celebrate these days, and so miss a great deal of pleasure, I think. But the people of whom I write always make a great deal of such occasions, and often got up very funny amusements" (IV, 218). Invariably, the occasions when all of the family is present are warm and happy and strengthen family ties. If a member has been away from the fold, the gathering reminds him of the support and happiness that is to be found there. In Alcott's work, only males leave the fold; the females are educated by their mothers in such a way as to realize the foolishness of such an endeavor. The males must leave to carry out their duties in the economic and political realms; the females, being of the domestic sphere, remain at home. The message is simply told. The family unit, the most successful and important institution in society, offers the bond of love and the motivation for labor. The wayward member senses the meaninglessness of his waywardness, and

10. Suddenly Tilly threw down the axe, flung open the door, and ran straight into the arms of the bear. *An Old-Fashioned Thanksgiving, Etc.,* Vol. 6.

the celebration symbolizes the family, particularly the love
that has been missing from his life.

Such is the case in "Kate's Choice," where the sons "wanted
to be something better, so they went away one after the other
to make their way in the world. All worked hard, got rich, lived
splendidly, and forgot as far as possible the old life and the dull
old place they came from" (III, 135). But Kate recognizes the
mistake and brings them together for Christmas for a rediscov-
ery of family ties. Kate is an "angel" who makes the others realize that their family ties can renew their lives.

The disruption of a holiday celebration is due to the absense
or death of the mother who would have ordinarily organized
the festivities. Through the disruption, the family members inevitably realize how much their family, especially their mother,
and the opportunity to be together mean to them. In this variation, some other member of the family (usually a child) takes
the responsibility to organize the festivities, determined to carry
on the sense of family. Alcott follows this formula in "An Old-
Fashioned Thanksgiving" (VI, 7-36), the title story of Volume
Six of the *Scrap-Bag*.

Both "Tessa's Surprises" (I, 35-57) and "Tilly's Christmas"
(I, 123-133), discussed in chapter 2, center around the holiday/
family celebration theme. In this case, the holiday is Christmas,
and since both families are poor, the children expect no gifts.
Yet Christmas is important, for it represents a time for their
families to strengthen their bonds of love. Both insist on trying
to celebrate it traditionally. Tessa will become the mother-sub-
stitute and provide the strength from which the other children
and the father can draw. Tilly's determination inspires Christian
kindness from a stranger. Each family celebrates Christmas after
a fashion, and, to repeat the cliché from "An Old-Fashioned
Thanksgiving," although the families are poor in money, they
are rich in love. The reader assumes, even though their futures
appear abysmal, that with love and family they will survive.

It is understood that the mother upholds the standards and
sets the moral tone for the rest of the family. She teaches this
way of life to her daughters, who set the moral tone for the
young men who court them. The only exception to this ideal
is the social butterfly, and, usually, she recognizes her mistake

and thus deserves the hand of the strong and honest man who
has been waiting for her to reform.

In "What A Shovel Did" (V, 154-167) Kate sets the proper
moral tone for Richard, her admirer, by insisting that he dedicate himself to a noble profession and that he show some evidence of his ability to succeed at it. She allows Richard no
compromises. When he finally comes to her, successful, she
says, "Richard, I was afraid you had gone down as so many
disappointed young men go when their ambitious hopes fail;
but I am so glad, so proud to see in your face that you still
work and wait, like a brave and honest man" (165).

Rose in *Rose in Bloom* holds out such standards for Charlie,
a charming cousin who courts her. He is attractive and intelligent but also self-indulgent and lazy; furthermore, he is a party
boy, one of the few Good Bad Boys (to borrow Leslie Fielder's
term) in all of Alcott's fiction. He has no patience with Rose's
plans to renovate her large city homes for apartments for poor,
respectable women, but she maintains she will never give up
"doing what I know is right." Rose admits she is particular, and
looks for "strength" and "goodness" and other "old-fashioned"
characteristics in prospective mates.

Although Rose is attracted to him, Charlie never measures
up. On New Year's Eve, he gets drunk, has an accident, and
returns to Rose, realizing his defeat. Alcott describes the failure
of the ideal:

> As she sat there with hidden eyes, Rose felt that some-
> thing dear to her was dead for ever. The ideal, which all
> women cherish, look for, and too often think they have
> found when love glorifies a mortal man, is hard to give
> up, especially when it comes in the likeness of the first
> lover who touches a young girl's heart. Rose had just be-
> gun to feel that perhaps this cousin, despite his faults,
> might yet become the hero that he sometimes looked;
> and the thought that she might be his inspiration was
> growing sweet to her, although she had not entertained
> it until very lately. Alas, how short the tender dream had
> been, how rude the awakening! how impossible it would
> be ever again to surround that fallen figure with all the

romance of an innocent fancy, or gift it with the high at-
tributes beloved by a noble nature![22]

Although Rose gives Charlie one more chance, he fails to redeem himself. Alcott punishes him with death and eventually
marries Rose off to another cousin, Mac, who is unglamorous,
but steadfast and true. Since he possesses the qualities that
Rose demands, he earns her love, and in a passionate scene rare
in Alcott fiction, Rose throws herself in his arms, "clinging
there in eloquent silence, while he held her close; feeling with
a thrill of tender triumph, that his was no longer little Rose,
but a loving woman, ready to live and die for him."[23]

Even though the young women set the moral standard for
men, the reader must not assume that they arrive at their state
of near perfection without a struggle. In fact, the most outstanding of Alcott heroines, Jo in *Little Women*, is memorable
because her struggle to attain perfection is so difficult. Her temper is uncontrollable, her emotions tempestuous, her personality changeable.

Most of the young women are working to rid themselves of
weaknesses, and, as Marmee in *Little Women* says, that task
will be lifelong. There are a few Good Good girls in Alcott's
fiction who have already "arrived." These young women, who
are saint-like in their perfection, are created in the tradition of
Little Eva in Harriet Beecher Stowe's *Uncle Tom's Cabin*. The
traditional Good Good girls have certain recognizable features
that have been described by Anne Tropp Trensky.[24] They are
often without one or both parents, thus suggesting an aura of
holiness. Their mothers are often pious and frail, and their
fathers are usually intensely devoted to them, with "an affection often verging on the erotic." The girls have a transforming
supernatural spiritual beauty, pale skin, and golden curls. They
usually suffer great pain, and if not rescued by protective
adults, ultimately die.

Alcott's "little women" fall within the saintly child tradition.
Anne Trensky explains that the moral development of the girls
comprises the story: Meg overcomes her need for a rich, fashionable life, Jo learns to control her temper, and Amy conquers her
vanity, willfulness, and selfishness.[25] Beth is the angel, "self sac-

rificing, piously humble and uncomplaining." But in the tradition of the pure saintly child, she must die.

The portraits of children in the *Scrap-Bag* stories also fall within the tradition of the saintly child. With one exception, they fall within Trensky's second category of the child who is potentially perfect. They may not attain perfection, as Trensky suggests they must, but we have no doubt that they will keep trying, being inspired by "wise and loving teachers," usually their mothers but sometimes maiden aunts.

The single portrait of the unequivocally saintly child in the *Scrap-Bags* appears in "My Little School Girl" (V, 141-153). The story records in a first-person narrative the passing encounters an old lady has with the young girl, who has "happy blue eyes" dimples in the ruddy cheeks, and the innocent expression which makes a young girl so sweet an object to old eyes" (142). She is a "good, sweet child" who always shares willingly, returns kind favors, and sets a cheerful, loving example for her friends. In the tradition of the saintly child stories, she dies. The story is puzzling because we have no idea what brought about her death. There is no suggestion of her saving others, although she does set a good example for other children. She is simply an example of the "dying maiden [who] is so highly regarded as the quintessence of female virtue, a being literally too good for this world."[26] If the narrator fails to despair, it is only because the little schoolgirl is sure to receive her place in heaven.

Sandra Gilbert and Susan Gubar's modern interpretation perceives Beth's death—and undoubtedly they would also include "My Little School Girl"—as a kind of suicide, typical of genteel women who "kill themselves . . . into art objects: slim, pale, passive beings whose 'charms' eerily recalled the snowy, porcelain immobility of the dead." They conclude that Beth March's sister Amy, in her "artful" way, really belongs in the same category, "and together these two heroines constitute complementary halves of the emblematic 'beautiful woman' whose *death*, thought Edgar Allan Poe, is unquestionably the most poetical topic in the world."[27]

But this perception is born out of the imposition of contemporary standards on nineteenth-century writing. The emphasis on such a figure is disproportionate. In fact, although there are plenty of young women in Alcott's writing who are striving for moral perfection, there are only two in her fiction of the type that Gilbert and Gubar describe above—Beth and the little schoolgirl. Although these portraits may suggest the romanticization of death, it seems that the significance of these angel-women is slight.

Indeed, the Little Eva type has taken on near mythic proportions in contemporary analyses of nineteenth-century writing. She is the central and initial image of Ann Douglas's study, and her type plays a central role in Gilbert and Gubar's study. Little Eva, who exemplifies religious faith and devoutness, is essentially decorative. And yet we have seen how Alcott and other nineteenth-century female authors rejected that role for women. Indeed, if we consider only the *Scrap-Bag* stories, it is a portrait of young women as vigorous and active that prevails. We have seen in our discussion in the last chapter how freedom of movement, exercise, health, and vibrancy constitute the ideal for Alcott. Although she acquiesced briefly in her portrait of the ethereal child in "My Little School Girl" to the fascination with romanticized death, her major thrust is certainly toward the healthy and wholesome young woman. If those women are attempting a moral perfection that puts them in the category of saintly, they are aided in their striving for perfection by the physical vigor and stamina they bring to their quest.

The potentially perfect child is often either an orphan or a member of a single-parent family. The orphans usually attach themselves to a family in some way, often as a servant who earns his or her way into the family circle. Of the sixty stories in the *Scrap-Bags*, nine include descriptions of single-parent families and fourteen include portraits of orphans.)

In the case of the single-parent family stories, the young daughters, occasionally the sons, assume the responsibility of the deceased mother or father—none of the single-parent families in Alcott's fiction is the result of divorce. The moral code of labor, love, and hope/cheerfulness defines the course of action for the child. Through what are often herculean efforts of labor, motivated by love, the daughter is able to meet her goal. The family feeling is more poignant because one parent is missing. The family members cope, however pitifully, striving to compensate for the missing parent. The family's fragility underscores the value of normal family life.

It is through the women that Alcott affirms the value of the traditional family. The mother, at the center of the family circle, guides the father/husband and children. The grandmother represents the "institution" of women's sphere. The young woman being courted sets both the tone for the relationship and the goals for the man who wishes her hand. And the young daughters prepare for the promise of destiny by learning their roles, taking them seriously, and educating themselves in a practical and complete way.

THE MAIDEN AUNT AND THE
REINFORCEMENT OF FAMILY VALUES

The maiden aunt in the *Scrap-Bag* stories is a skillful nurse and healer, a gentle teacher, a beloved helper and assistant, and an informal therapist who advises family members and manipulates their behavior in such a way as to bring greater harmony to family relationships. In this way, although not directly in the family circle, she is of it. Because she is outside the family, she brings objectivity that allows her to assess problems and recommend solutions. Her presence reinforces the family's moral values.

We have already discussed in chapter 2 how Aunt Pen in "Patty's Patchwork" (I, 193-215) teaches Patty the discipline of labor when she insists that Patty continue to work on a comforter, even after she learns that her baby sister—for whom the comforter was intended—has died a few days after birth. In the same objective way, Aunt Jane in "Patty's Place" (IV, 161-186) helps the Murray family to see that they have been taking their servant, Patty, for granted. She has suggested Patty for the position, encouraged her to do her best, promising her full reward for her labor. By encouraging the family to show their affection for Patty, Aunt Jane helps bring about her transfiguration. And her love transforms the Murray family as well—all through the doing of the maiden aunt.

Occasionally the maiden aunts know what behaviors to recommend because, although single, they have reared families of
their own. Often in the fiction, as with maiden aunts in real
life, their single state was chosen through what Barbara Welter
calls "fidelity to some high mission."[28] Usually this high mission is devotion to another family member who is ill or needs
help in some way. This devotion leads to fulfillment that is as
rewarding for the maiden aunt as married life would have been.

Aunt Betsey in "The Children's Joke" (I, 67-90) knows what
is wrong with the Fairbairn family, with whom she resides, because "sister Betsey had brought up a flock of motherless brothers and sisters and done it wisely and well, though she never got
any praise or thanks for it, and never expected any for doing
her duty faithfully" (70). The Fairbairn children "had everything heart could desire." Alcott sums up the family problems:

> With the best intentions in the world, Mr. and Mrs. Fair-
> bairn were spoiling their children by constant fault-finding,
> too many rules, and too little sympathy with the active
> young souls and bodies under their care. As Harry said,
> they were ordered about, corrected and fussed over from
> morning till night, and were getting so tired of it that the
> most desperate ideas began to enter their heads. (69)

When in idle chatter the children suggest switching roles with
the parents so that they may gain an understanding of what
they are putting their children through, Aunt Betsey supports
the idea: "Merely let the children do as they like for one day
and have full power over you. Let them plan your duties and
pleasures, order your food, fix your hours, and punish or reward you as they think proper. You must promise entire obedience, and keep the agreement till night" (73). Feeling they
have nothing to lose, the parents agree to this scheme. What results is the first description I have seen of the twentieth-century
therapeutic method of role-playing—in nineteenth-century fiction. Alcott concludes the story by having the children put the
parents to bed at an unreasonably early hour. This mission accomplished, the children speculate about the success of their

venture, and Aunt Betsey promises victories. The story criticizes
the demands that the rigors of various social rituals such as dress
and manners place upon the children. And, once again, from
her objective point and from her practical experience, the maid-
en aunt is in a position to bring about changes that immediate
family members cannot.

The role of the maiden aunt is, of course, the posture that
the author uses to present the *Scrap-Bag* volumes. The perception of the maiden aunt as learned and rational was one that
had been carefully cultivated by earlier writers such as Lydia
Marie Child, whose Aunt counseled her nieces and nephews on
diverse topics, and Caroline Hentz's Aunt Patty, whose clever-
ness inspired the young Worth children. The role of maiden
aunt was an intellectual but safe one because it allowed freedom for intellectual endeavors but did not prove women as un-
fit for feminine pursuits; the intellectual role could never, after
all, be severed from virtue and duty.

This fictional role modeled on her predecessors was, in fact,
a role Alcott assumed in real life. Like Aunt Betsey in "The
Children's Joke," she had brought up a family, construing it as
"doing her duty faithfully." For an unmarried woman to serve
such a role was an example of a "noble end" that Alcott wrote
of so often. The women who were born during the decades that
Alcott was writing the *Scrap-Bag* stories, the 1860s and 1870s,
married less than any others before and after. Over 10 percent
of women born between 1860 and 1880 never married, thereby
avoiding exclusively domestic vocations.[29] The historian Barbara Welter has pointed out that, although marriage was the
proper and best state for women, it wasn't absolutely essential.
"The women's magazines," she writes, "tried to remove the
stigma from being an 'old maid' "[30] They advised that it was
better not to be married than to be unhappily married. These
maiden ladies could perform the same duties that the maiden
aunts in the *Scrap-Bag* do—care for the sick; teach the young,
either in their classroom or their writing; and support various
causes that married women could not because of family commitments. To the extent that they were extraordinary in the
performance of such duties, they were "absolved from the necessity of marriage."[31]

THE SINGLE WOMAN AND NOBLE ENDS

In the discussion of social butterflies, we have already considered how much Alcott admires the women in "My Girls" who devote themselves to noble ends. Because these women are dedicated to noble ends, they cannot be social butterflies, even though four of the six are apparently from well-to-do families. Not vicarious consumers, they engage in different types of productive labor. None is married: three have chosen a career over marriage; a fourth has devoted herself to helping her father's business and to the care of her father and siblings; another has devoted herself to "private charities"; and the last is a young black girl who is "making her way" in the white world of the North. Two of the women died young: one, the lawyer, apparently from overwork; the other from "saving the most forlorn of our sister women in a private way." The three "girls" in medicine, art, and law "chose" those careers, the implication being that they decided against marriage. Since all of them work very hard at their careers, Alcott implies they probably would not have had time for a family. Alcott tells us that several of them, as was true of so many nineteenth-century feminists, had fathers who encouraged them to develop themselves intellectually. She writes: "Fortunately ["A"] had a father who did not think marriage the only thing a woman was created for, but was ready to help his daughter in the work she had chosen, merely desiring her to study as faithfully and thoroughly as a man, if she undertook the profession that she might be an honor to it" (9).

All three of the career women are successful, but Alcott makes no pretensions about the difficulties of their choice. The study of medicine has for "A" been "a solitary lot," full of "hard work" and prejudice. As we already noted, the study and practice of law has led to the death of "E." Alcott quotes a friend who says of "E's" death: " 'She was a royal girl, and did all her work in a royal way. She broke down suddenly, just as she had begun to taste the ineffable sweetness of peace and rest, following a relative life-time of battle and toil" (20). If these career women sacrificed, it was not in vain, for Alcott tells us that each one has "cleared the way for those who come after her, and proved that women have not only the right but the ability to sit upon the bench as well as stand at the bar of justice" (21).

"F," the young black woman, also "clears the way" for others, not only of her sex but also of her race. She has managed to learn to read and write and spends all her free time reading to educate herself more fully, which the reader assumes will help free her both psychologically and intellectually.

The portraits from "My Girls" that are closest to those presented in her *Scrap-Bags* are of "D" and "B." "D" tries a career in the theatre finds it wanting (as Christie Devon in *Work* had) and gives it up to become her father's clerk and to care for her brothers and sisters. And "B," who works very hard at her art, has opened a free art school "for those who cared to come." (Could this portrait be based on her sister May?) Alcott tells us that the artist wants to share and teach—two strongly feminine virtues. She writes, "For with her, as with most who *earn* their good things, the generous desire to share them with others is so strong it is sure to blossom out in some way, blessing as it has been blessed" (13).

There is another more famous work in which Alcott espouses education and careers for women for self-realization. *Jo's Boys* reflects Alcott's interests in women's rights, and "higher education and a professional career as the means for a woman's self realization."[32] Although the girls in *Little Women* become wives and manage to give up, alter, or repress their youthful ambitions, in *Jo's Boys* their daughters fulfill these ambitions. A change in emphasis and direction for education can be traced through the three March novels. The shift can be explained, in part, by Alcott's perception of herself as author. When she was composing *Little Women* in 1868, she was trying to capture a mass market, as her diaries so revealingly show, and she was careful to fulfill conventional expectations about women's roles. When she composed *Jo's Boys* over ten years later, she was America's favorite juvenile author with a commitment to encouraging young women to pursue their ambitions. As a result, Alcott portrays Nan in *Jo's Boys* as "an example of an individual woman finding fulfillment in a chosen career" as well as "a vociferous spokeswoman for women's voting rights."[33]

How does the reader reconcile the portraits of the real-life women presented in "My Girls," who are closer to that of Nan in *Jo's Boys*, with the fictional girls and women in the other *Scrap-Bag* stories? The women in the stories operate within the domestic sphere. The women in "My Girls" have made other choices; even the more traditional of the six have departed to some degree from the usual choices of domesticity.

The answer lies in conceptualizing the roles not as separate spheres but as existing along a continuum. The popularization of the concept of "woman's sphere" has underlined the dichotomy and overlooked the opportunites for continuity that the system actually offered. At one end of the scale are the traditional domestic roles and at the other are radical feminist roles. This conceptualization eliminates the necessity to categorize women in one sphere—domesticity—or another—radical feminism—recognizing instead that women, in their various roles, might move along the continuum. In fact, the work of recent scholars of women's social history suggests that many who operated within the domestic sphere worked in support of radical feminist notions. For instance, Carroll Smith-Rosenburg has shown how women in evangelically motivated reform societies sought active social roles, asserted female worth in a largely male world, and supported the creation of feminine loyalties to one another.[34]

Alcott's girls and women are somewhere in the middle of the continuum. They are domestic feminists who believe in preparing themselves for the coming crisis in women's destiny by doing the best they can with what they have to work with, but in the traditional roles. They reject the notion of woman as merely conspicuous consumer and displayer of her husband's wealth. They believe in equality for women but are willing to work within the system to achieve it. These women prepare for future opportunities by educating themselves properly in both practical and traditionally masculine subjects. The women in "My Girls" and Nan in *Jo's Boys* have broadened their horizon through education and public experience. Exceptional enough to move out of traditional women's roles, these educated women have moved farther along the continuum to radical feminism. The system allowed them to do so, partly because they retained their single status and did not try to combine a career and marriage. The one who comes closest to attaining both, the physician, adopts a child so that she may have a sense of family. In "clearing the way" these women, Alcott realizes, help define all women as capable of working in public professions as well as in the home.

Barbara Welter has defined the ways in which women were described as ruled by the heart rather than the mind and therefore trapped in anti-intellectualism. She points out that innocence often was equivalent to a lack of knowledge, that women's education stressed masculine authority and feminine submission and inferiority, and that men were perceived of as reasonable while women were primarily intuitive—in short, that women were nonintellectual.[35] When Alcott began portraying women that were part of the popular culture of the day as intellectual, subject to reason, and interested in a "tough" education, she took an important first step in allowing women to move freely along the continuum. These portraits were consistent with the lives of intellectual women she knew—Lydia Marie Child, Elizabeth Peabody, Ednah Cheney, and Margaret Fuller.

In the fiction, given an audience of children and adults who wanted to shape gentry ideals, it was wisest for Alcott to keep the scale balanced in the middle. Doing so guaranteed her stories' acceptance by the editors of the magazines and popularity with the reading public. Given the opportunity to voice personal opinions (as she did in "My Girls"), Alcott could move further along the scale toward radical feminism by portraying strong intellectual women.

ALCOTT'S WOMEN AND THE CULT OF TRUE WOMANHOOD

Any women of the nineteenth century who possessed the virtues of piety, purity, submissiveness, and domesticity had achieved the state of True Womanhood. As Barbara Welter explains in her analysis of True Womanhood, "religion or piety was the core of woman's virtue, the source of her strength."[36] And purity was as essential as piety to a True Woman. Welter writes, "The marriage night was the single great event of a

woman's life, when she bestowed her greatest treasure upon
her husband, and from that time on was completely dependent
upon him, an empty vessel, without legal or emotional existence
of her own."[37] For this great moment, the true woman main-
tained her purity; in doing so she demonstrated her moral superiority and power over men. Women, once married, were expected to be passive and submissive. And finally a true woman's
place was at home, and domesticity was among the most prized
virtues. In her role at home, the woman brought men back to
God, made the home so cheerful that men would not want to
go elsewhere, nursed her husband and children, completed
needlework, cultivated flowers, read judiciously (from morally
acceptable works), cooked, and carried out the necessary household tasks.

There is no question that Alcott perceives the women in her
fiction as True Women. Certainly they are pure and domestic,
but they differ from the True Women discussed above. Alcott
was reared when the cult of True Womanhood was in flower—
Welter defines the period from 1820 to 1860, Alcott was born
in 1832—but as she wrote, women's roles began to change. It
is probably not overstating the case to say that by illustrating
the changes in her fiction, she helped bring them about. To discuss some of the changes, let us consider Alcott's handling of
the "cardinal virtues."

The True Woman was pious. Alcott's women are pious only
in the sense that they are conscientiously exact. They acknowledge a final accounting, but at the same time their emphasis is
on following the golden rule for the rewards it brings in life,
not out of a sense of religious devotion. Alcott reflects this
position in her moral code of labor, love, and hope. A pious
woman would have emphasized faith instead of hope and
placed it first in the moral code.

The True Woman was pure. Alcott's women are pure.
Through their virtue, their source of power, they control both
men and children. Closely associated with their virtue is their
innocence, which all young women in the *Scrap-Bag* stories
possess.

The True Woman was submissive. Alcott's women choose
their roles rather than submit to them, a difference with vast

implications. Alcott's women understand these roles can work
to their advantage: their place in the domestic sphere is a position of power rather than weakness. The notion of working to
attain ends by submitting and thereby making the husband so
happy and contented that he (who wields the power and exer-
cises authority) will grant whatever the woman desires apparently rankled Alcott. Her women do what they wish, assuming
their husbands will agree. The women in the *Scrap-Bag* stories
are not submissive, yet they remain feminine, which they perceive as a source of strength.

Alcott's women understand that they control their destiny—
they change behavior and solve problems, decide the best childrearing approaches. In all fairness, it must be acknowledged that
the women in Alcott's fiction hold their power, in part, because
of the relative absence of men. The men who are present are
curiously insipid. Rather than taking an active role in shaping
their children's behavior, they allow themselves to be acted
upon by their wives. Daughters even seem to manage their
fathers. Tessa Bennari in "Tessa's Surprises" assumes sole responsibility for the family's Christmas festivities, while the
father contributes next to nothing. The father in *Little Women*
serves as a chaplain in the war for nearly half the novel; while
his return is an occasion for joy, it changes the family activities
very little. The men in the fiction do not oppose what the wom-
en want to do. At their strongest, they support them. Ellen in
"Cupid and Chow-Chow" has faith that the model her husband
presents for her son will be consistent with her own beliefs.
This support of fathers and/or husbands is seen as an important
element in the lives of nineteenth-century feminists, as several
recent studies have shown.[38] Alcott is, in a sense, ignoring the
masculine role. To some extent, this is probably fair, because
the men, as tradition had it, played only a small role in rearing
the children, and the women, who had the power in the family,
chose not to move into the men's sphere. For them the political
and economic realms promised little. As we have seen, the greatest opportunities were the personal and social ones developed
through preparation and education within the family.

The True Woman was domestic. Alcott's women are domestic: they make the home cheerful so the men will want to be

there; they nurse their children and husbands; they do patch-work and needlework; they cultivate vegetables and appreciate flowers; they read and keep diaries; and they cook, clean, and care for the children. They do not, however, carry out a religious mission in the traditional sense of the word, which was primary among the cardinal virtues of the True Woman. They are faithful to themselves first. The domestic situation does not formulate their identity; it is established before they marry. The sense of mission in choosing the domestic way overrides the mundaneness of the domestic tasks, ascribing to them a great opportunity to shape the destiny of their children.

The girls in Alcott's fiction reflect the dilemma of the American girl in the nineteenth century—to be equally bold and innocent.[39] The girls are almost always obedient. Their disobedience, when it occasionally occurs, is benign, usually resulting in pleasant surprises or extra niceties that bring joy and a sense of togetherness to the family, if only briefly.

Perhaps their biggest challenge is to develop self-control, the conflict that makes the characterization of Jo in *Little Women* so memorable. The girls attempt to control selfishness, laziness, and pettiness. They control themselves to improve themselves and thereby to create opportunities. They are bold enough to dare to accomplish the difficult, the unusual, yet they maintain the traditional feminine values. In doing so, they prepare for the choices they assume they will have as adults.

The most striking quality in the girls and women in the *Scrap-Bag* stories is their strength: they think, they reason, they decide, they act, and they work very hard. They overcome adversity. They use their intuition to supplement their reason, not in place of it. They are not fragile, submissive, or superficial, and Alcott chides those who are.

By characterizing women as strong and thoughtful, Alcott helps to set the stage for the women of the next generation who, like several of the women in "My Girls," chose public vocations. A recent study of three women who chose public vocations—Lillian Wald, Crystal Eastman, and Emma Goldman—has shown how they worked diligently and independently at their chosen vocations, sometimes against great hostility.[40] They were supported by a network of other politically and pro-

fessionally active women, as earlier nineteenth-century women
had been supported in their work within the domestic sphere
by other women. Jane Addams is an example of the female
social workers of the generation that followed Alcott who took
the traditional concerns that women had for the proper education of youth out of the domestic sphere and into the streets.
In fact, Jane Addams supports the same causes for youth in her
work and writing that Alcott does in her short stories. Best
known for her work with Hull House, she also wrote a book
that dealt with the "conflict between man and industrial society, a conflict whose most severe effects fell upon youth."[41]
In that book, *The Spirit of Youth and the City Streets*, she focuses on the need for an "organic connection" between work
and play for youth, a theme that Alcott had emphasized earlier
in many of her stories.

From these women at the turn of the century who work to
improve society, it is only another step to the women of the
1920s that Paula Fass describes in *The Damned and the Beautiful* who question, criticize, and even rebel. The youth of the
1920s found the customs, manners, and fashions of society
hypocritical, and the women became as openly critical, vocal,
and rebellious as the men. Their questioning attitude led to a
rejection of the genteel values that Alcott was essentially supporting in her stories that were originally published in such
genteel magazines as *Youth's Companion* and *St. Nicholas*. But
her alteration of the cardinal virtues of the True Woman—from
pious to healthy-minded and faithful to self, from submissive
to assertive—provides a necessary link between the True Women
of the nineteenth century and the social activists and feminists
of the early twentieth century.

NOTES

1. Abby Alcott, quoted in Madelon Bedell, *The Alcotts* (New York:
Clarkson N. Potter, Inc., 1980), p. 285.
2. Chow-chow is an assortment of highly seasoned, pungent pickles.
3. Sandra M. Gilbert and Susan Gubar, *The Madwoman in the Attic*
(New Haven: Yale University Press, 1979).

4. Ibid., p. 64.

5. Daniel Scott Smith, "Family Limitation, Sexual Control and Domestic Feminism in Victorian America," *Feminist Studies*, 1 (Winter-Spring 1973), 40-57.

6. Smith, "Family Limitation," p. 53.

7. Nina Baym, *Woman's Fiction* (Ithaca, New York: Cornell University Press, 1978), p. 18.

8. Martha Saxton, *Louisa May* (New York: Avon Books, 1977), p. 327.

9. Alcott, *Rose in Bloom* (New York: Grosset and Dunlop, 1976), p. 47.

10. Ibid., p. 261.

11. Alcott, *Little Women* (New York: Collier Books, 1962), p. 116.

12. Ibid.

13. Alcott, *Rose in Bloom*, pp. 300-301.

14. Baym, *Woman's Fiction*, p. 28.

15. Ibid.

16. Ann Douglas, *The Feminization of American Culture* (New York: Avon Books, 1977). See chapter two, "Feminine Disestablishment," pp. 50-94.

17. Baym, *Woman's Fiction*, pp. 232-236.

18. Thorstein Veblen, *The Theory of the Leisure Class* (New York: New American Library, 1953), p. 126.

19. Alcott, *Little Women*, p. 96.

20. Ibid., pp. 96-97.

21. Madeleine B. Stern, *Louisa May Alcott* (Norman: University of Oklahoma Press, 1950), pp. 232-233.

22. Alcott, *Rose in Bloom*, p. 151.

23. Ibid., p. 321.

24. Anne Tropp Trensky, "The Saintly Child in Nineteenth-Century American Fiction," *Prospects*, I (1975), 389-413. Trensky traces portraits of the first type through the works of Fanny Fern (*Fern Leaves from Fanny's Port-Folio*, 1853), Elizabeth Oakes Smith (*The Newsboy*, 1854), Harriet Beecher Stowe (*Uncle Tom's Cabin*, 1852, and *Oldtown Folks*, 1868). The second type is more characteristic of Susan B. Warner's *The Wide, Wide World* (1850) and Martha Finley's *Elsie Dinsmore* (1868).

25. Ibid., p. 405.

26. Barbara Welter, *Dimity Convictions* (Athens: Ohio University Press, 1976), p. 11.

27. Gilbert and Gubar, *The Madwoman in the Attic*, p. 25.

28. Welter, *Dimity Convictions*, p. 37.

29. Nancy F. Cott and Elizabeth H. Pleck, eds., introductory com-

ments to Blanche Weisen Cook, "Female Support Networks and Political Activism," *A Heritage of Her Own* (New York: Simon and Schuster, 1979), p. 412.

30. Welter, *Dimity Convictions*, p. 37.

31. Ibid.

32. Niki Alpert McCurry, "Concepts of Childrearing and Schooling in the March Novels of Louisa May Alcott," Ph. D. Dissertation, Northwestern University, 1976, p. 101.

33. Ibid., pp. 99-100.

34. Carroll Smith-Rosenberg, "Beauty, the Beast, and the Militant Woman," *American Quarterly*, 23 (1971), 562-584.

35. Welter, *Dimity Convictions*, pp. 71-82.

36. Ibid., p. 22.

37. Ibid., pp. 23-24.

38. Robert E. Reigel, "Patterns of Nineteenth-Century Feminism," in Welter, *The Woman Question in American History* (Hinsdale, Illinois: The Dryden Press, 1973) and Susan Conrad, *Perish the Thought* (New York: Oxford University Press, 1976).

39. Welter, *Dimity Convictions*, p. 20.

40. Blanche Wiesen Cook, "Female Support Networks and Political Activism," *Chrysalis*, 3 (1977).

41. Joseph F. Kett, *Rites of Passage* (New York: Basic Books, Inc., 1977), p. 226.

5

Departures

The short stories in the six volumes of Louisa May Alcott's *Aunt Jo's Scrap-Bag* are the children's counterpart of that great body of essays, pamphlets, and books written in the nineteenth century by ministers and popular writers who gave advice to parents on how to rear their children. As such, they can tell us much about the attitudes and values that nineteenth-century parents held about their children and the proper way they should be reared, although, of course, they can tell us little about the actual practices parents engaged in. Although the stories are not as heavily didactic as earlier nineteenth-century tales, they are still formula stories that teach a moral lesson, however delicately that lesson is incorporated. As moral tales, they are part of a body of literature that was concerned with how those children should best be reared to fulfill their destiny in a land that offered great promise for their adult lives. As moral tales, they echoed the themes of youth counselors, who argued that childhood offered the best opportunities for parents to shape their children's behavior and that the mother was primarily responsible for this task.

As we have seen, the moral tale taught children the important lesson of self-control that led them to their proper social roles and conduct. The tales were published primarily in periodicals edited by men and women who hoped to guide the behavior of their readers according to traditional notions of genteel behavior. Although the editors were of the gentry social class, their periodicals and the stories that appeared in them, including Alcott's stories, spoke to both the poor and the rich. While it counseled acceptance of one's plight at the moment, at the same time it encouraged children to prepare for a better future and to make something of themselves. Alcott's stories met the editors' criteria, following the traditional formulas that showed children either surviving an ordeal or undergoing a change of heart that gave evidence of their willingness to strive for moral perfection.

The moral code imposed immense burdens on the children in the *Scrap-Bag* stories. Most of them strive to grow in grace by following a moral code of labor, love, and hope: industry is a good teacher, love makes industry worthwhile, and optimism brings a proper perspective to one's work and plight, however difficult it may be. The children who understand and operate by this demanding moral code are indeed outstanding; in fact, at times they appear to the modern reader as miniature adults who possess the wisdom of maturity, much as the portraits of earlier medieval artists characterized children as miniature adults. They retain their youthfulness through a sense of wonder and innocence. Their abilities are boundless, and at times they seem to lack an awareness of the difficulties of the tasks they face. Yet this sense of wonder is fleeting, and they proceed about their duty of accomplishing these nearly impossible tasks in a remarkably matter-of-fact way.

Alcott follows the beliefs of the romantics and the transcendentalists about the nature of children and portrays them as exceptionally wise. Through the development of their consciences, they have learned the lessons of self-control and are willing to subjugate themselves to a secondary position, placing the needs of others above their own, a remarkable feat considering that most of the children in the *Scrap-Bag* stories belong to that class Alcott calls "the silent poor" and therefore have pressing material needs of their own. Their insights are so perceptive that again and again they teach the adults around them, usually through example, the important lessons of life that are embodied in the moral code. They help adults see things in proper perspective, teaching the value of love and reminding adults of the solidarity that the family circle offers. Although there is some evidence that Alcott is attracted to the naughty child, having been one herself, for the most part her stories are those of potentially perfect children. Being quite exceptional, these children are educated in a manner consistent with their intelligence; their curriculum makes use of their own perceptions, implements the lessons of nature, and stresses the interconnectedness of the body and the mind.

The women in the *Scrap-Bag* stories are nearly as remarkable as the children. They are at the center of the household, and the family activities radiate from them. These women, who have primary responsibility for rearing the children, possess many of the characteristics of the "True Woman" of the domestic sphere: they devote themselves to others; their morality serves as a guide to husbands, fiancés, children, and friends; and they gather their strength from a support system of other women. Like the protagonists of many of the nineteenth-century domestic novels by women, Alcott's women develop their identity and act independently. They are not submissive; if they engage in what might be called typical female behavior it is because they choose to do so, not because it is forced on them. They take themselves and their responsibilities for childrearing very seriously and educate themselves in order to understand and to participate in the "coming crisis in women's destiny." Alcott and the characters in her stories have little respect for those women who refuse to take themselves seriously and for those who fail to devote themselves to "noble ends," such as the "social butterflies" who engage in meaningless social customs.

Both the children and women in Alcott's stories have great strength and vitality and an eagerness to participate in the activities of the world. They take themselves and their education seriously in order to prepare for the opportunities they will have so that they can, as Alcott would say, fulfill their destiny —the children as future citizens, the young women as wives, mothers, social activists, and, as some of Alcott's later stories suggest, perhaps even as career women in the public sphere.

Considering these generalizations about Alcott's short stories and the roles that the children and women play in them, what are the implications for the place of Alcott's *Scrap-Bag* in the overall body of writing on children and women in nineteenth-century America?

First of all, let us consider Alcott's personal life and her career as author. In these stories Alcott, as Aunt Jo, is operating as teacher, a role she had forsaken in the classroom but that she could never forsake in her writing. Although Jo, in the guise of storyteller, distracts us momentarily from educational concerns, it is Jo as teacher who emerges in the *Scrap-Bag* tales. We are tempted to be lured away from the educational motives by our knowledge that Jo's real-life counterpart was a woman who abhorred teaching, claimed to have little success at it, and perceived it as something to keep her from starving until she could earn her way as a writer. Yet when she took up the pen she modeled herself after Maria Edgeworth, the writer of moral tales who was popularly considered one of the foremost writers on education.

It is the passionate nature of teacher concerned with molding the character of her students that we see here. The moral tale is, after all, the literary counterpart to the adult childrearing literature. Like the authors of those advice-giving essays, Alcott was concerned with counseling children on how they could develop their character. Like them, she believed that a configuration of moral qualities were gradually molded in each child. Like them, she believed that the fundamental mark of character was "a strenuous will" that was dominated by self-restraint and self-control. Like them, she thought the changing conditions of her time made it necessary to provide a way to bridge the gap between traditional values and new conditions.

Granted, Alcott perceived herself as writer. Yet to reach an audience she agreed to so many concessions that she inhibited her art. She agreed to the genre of the moral tale traditionally published in children's periodicals. She agreed to a formula that prescribed a limited range of characterizations and conflicts consistent with the motto that called for forming minds, preparing hearts, and molding characters. She agreed to a maximum length of 3,000 words, which limited her power to dramatize the human condition she so keenly perceived. And there were the unwritten, less obvious, constraints. Her stories must always assume that the future would be better; the definition of the character as shaper of environment kept them from being realistic. Alcott felt keenly enough the power of her environment to shape her career, yet she could never acquiesce in the stories to that reality.

Perhaps Alcott limited herself even more than she realized
in spelling out the moral code of Labor, Love, and Hope in her
stories. The code had all the elements of a teacher's lesson plan.
It was simple and systematic, able to be reinforced again and
again, and yet adaptable to rich complexities and subtleties on
necessary occasions. As a former teacher herself, she must have
come to realize that internalization of the moral code and for-
mation of character were more likely to succeed in structured
than casual environments. One thinks of the diagrams of the-
oretical models that teachers so often construct to guide their
instruction and to suggest a framework. Alcott's model would
work out as a triangle with the elements of the code at the three
points with arrows indicating the direction of movement both
ways:

Labor

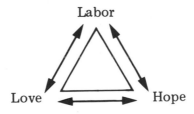

Love   Hope

The diagram reveals immediately that the subject matter of the
stories is limited by the definition of the code. The code is a
closed system, ultimately inhibiting the invention of conflict,
characterization, setting, and theme necessary for great art.
While it could deal with tragic subjects such as death, loneliness,
and poverty, its treatment must always be moral, excluding any
subjects relating to evil. And by definition the system must succeed; Alcott never portrayed any failures. Her stories are success stories and indicate a domination of life by the individual.
The goal was a moral life, the method of attainment the moral
code. She must have at times felt compelled to break the bonds
of the code, and indeed, her gothic thrillers represent the code
destroyed. Writing them surely had a cathartic effect, yet she
refused to acknowledge them publicly, publishing them anonymously instead.

In portraying this code, Alcott was in fact describing the
code that she tried to live by, with its great demand for self-
discipline and its emphasis on love and duty. Her journals reveal

again and again that it had helped her to cope with poverty, illness, even death, and to bear the great personal sacrifice she
made in putting her obligations to love and duty before her art.
The sections of her journals that she destroyed most certainly
must have revealed an inconsistency with the moral code.
Rather than admit those inconsistencies, she erased them, elimi-
nating or at least reducing discrepancies between her public
persona and private self.

And what of Alcott's *Scrap-Bag* collection? The stories themselves reflect the temperament and experiences of their time.
They were mostly written and published in the decade of the
1870s, a time of changing expectations for both women and
children. Women were beginning to demand the vote and fuller
participation in the public sphere. Alcott's stories are domestic
tales, yet the women are less submissive and more independent
than the "true women" who were at the center of the traditional family circle.

The changes that we see in the role of women reflect those
of the period of transition that comes after the full realization
of the role of women within the domestic sphere that Nancy F
Cott defines (from 1780 to 1835) and Barbara Welter discusses
(from 1820 to 1860). This period of transition witnessed what
Cott rightly calls two contradictory visions of women's relation
to society: "the ideology of domesticity, which gave women a
limited and sex-specific role to play, primarily in the home;
and feminism, which attempted to remove sex-specific limits
on women's opportunities and capacities."[1] Alcott's stories
conceptualize how a less sex-specific role might work itself out
in an idealized family setting. In that setting the young woman
is, as we have seen, independent, with a sense of identity that
she brings to the marriage. The women in Alcott's stories create
and choose their options rather than submit to them. They
make decisions, largely those regarding the domestic realm and
the rearing of children, with which the husbands concur and
which they never question. They marry for love rather than
duty, obligation, or arrangement. They are knowledgeable
about their status in society and cognizant of political reform
activities, such as the woman's suffrage movement and of the
necessity for increased educational opportunities for women.

In short, they have a sense of autonomy, a necessary ingredient in women's search for equality.

Alcott's language challenges women to prepare to lead the way. Her attempt to deal with the contradictions of the ideologies of the domestic sphere and of feminism resolve themselves in the portrayal of domestic feminism, in which women assert themselves within traditional frames of reference. Even the most revolutionary of the nineteenth-century feminists argued that it was a wise procedure for women to work on the domestic front as well as the more public, nontraditional ones.

Several scholars have discussed the contradictions of such a conceptualization. For example, Thomas H. Pauly in *"Ragged Dick* and *Little Women:* Idealized Homes and Unwanted Marriages,"* has argued that Alcott and Horatio Alger have created protagonists whose values, interests, and attitudes "become aligned with positions which militate against marriage, thus unwittingly undermining the very institution these writers are consciously striving to recommend."[2] Alcott is arguing that, in order for women's roles within the domestic sphere to be fulfilling rather than limiting, the women must have a sense of autonomy. It is clear that, if given independence, the women in her stories will choose to strengthen the institution of marriage rather than undermine it. At the same time, the *Scrap-Bag* stories acknowledge that there are other opportunities for self-actualization than those of wife and mother within the domestic sphere. An obvious example is that of the maiden aunt, a role that Alcott portrays and that is suggested in her role as presenter of the *Scrap-Bag* tales and professional storyteller. This posture works from the domestic realm but moves out of it to the public professional realm. The descriptions of women she admires in "My Girls" suggest public vocations outside the domestic realm that anticipate those of Elizabeth and Emily Blackwell in medicine and Jane Addams in social work. Rather than being contradictory, it seems that Alcott is being practical and, in doing so, is following a great tradition of American thinkers and writers who believed that practicality pays. Domestic feminism was a practical compromise, but a definite improvement on the status quo.

As American artists working in other fields had adopted prac-

tical measures and designs for aesthetic ends, so the moral tale
is itself a very practical application of a literary art form. If
children were to enjoy literature, they should learn as they enjoyed. With the practicality of the moral tale comes a certain
consistency; these independent and wise children, who are so
exceptional that they educate adults, cannot be perverted into
submissive adult women who acquiesce to what the patriarchal
system calls out for them. They must instead be independent
decision-makers who fulfill the promise of their destiny not by
submitting to it but by participating in it and therefore controlling it, at least to some degree.

The portrayal of children, too, reflects the temperament of
the time. The obligations of the moral code that Alcott portrays suggest an attitude toward children that is consistent with
that of the "moderates" described by Philip Greven in his recent
study of childrearing practices in early America. *The Protestant
Temperament: Patterns of Child-rearing, Religious Experience,
and the Self in Early America*. In contrast to Perry Miller, who
has interpreted the early American experience through the Puritan mind and religious doctrine, Greven suggests that there were
operating in early America several distinctive expressions of
temperament—inner experiences—that called forth different approaches to childrearing. In contrast to the "evangelicals," who
sought to break the will of their children and the "genteel" who
were more interested in developing their children's self-assertion
than self-control, the "moderates" attempted to bend the will
of their children. Moderates took for granted the innocent nature of their infant children and sought to develop their self-
control gradually throughout childhood with moderate discipline and voluntary obedience. Greven writes:

> Throughout the centuries, love and domestic affection
> were the bonds that united parents and children in the
> families of moderates. . . . But love was still not . . . the
> dominant theme. Duty was of even greater significance
> as a motif of the moderate temperament.
>
> Although children in the families of moderates grew
> up feeling that their own wills were free and that their
> compliance with the wills of their parents was voluntary,

they grew up also with an equally intense sense of limits
upon their freedom expressed by the term "duty."
"Duty"—which almost always balanced "love"— was a
word that implied subordination, deference, and respect.[3]

This description captures the family situation in the Alcott
stories precisely. Although the children are portrayed as members of the class of "the silent poor" and they therefore are of
a different class from the well-to-do Winthrops and Adamses
that Greven so frequently quotes from, their lives are moder-
ated by love and duty. Children understand that their sense
of duty shapes their connections with their family, and it is
this sense of obligation that binds families together. Developed
by the nurturance of self-control, duty expresses the obligations of these children to their parents, and parents to children.
These obligations establish and sustain a proper distance between family members and thus balance the affection and love,
which often threaten to be overwhelming. The sense of obligation developed through love and duty leads to a self-denial of
appetites and passions best accomplished through unremitting
industriousness.

The children of one-parent families feel these obligations of
connection even more strongly than those of "normal" families.
The lack of one parent places the family out of balance, and the
child realizes that he or she must attempt to compensate for the
deficiencies and rectify the imbalances. Sons become substitute
father-figures and daughters substitute mother-figures in a manner that seems more typical of children in single-parent families
of our time. The orphans often attempt to find a place in a regular family by proving their worth through carrying out the obligations of duty which will earn them the right of love. The
number of orphans and children with a single living parent is
extremely high in the stories, perhaps because Alcott's commitment
to the ordeal formula forced her to choose characters whose
life situations were extremely stressful. These children do not
fit into the definition of childhood as a period of protected de-
pendency within the home.

Although Bronson's notion of children as redeemers had

clearly been in advance of his time, Louisa's portrayal of children in the *Scrap-Bag* stories as potentially perfect is closer to
the perception of children commonly held as the century neared
its end, a time that had been characterized as the era of "the
child redeemer."⁴ As we have seen, the children whom Alcott
portrays truly redeem: they often deliver adults from sin and its
penalties, they fulfill the dreams their parents hold for them,
and they make amends or compensate for the moral deficiencies
of those around them.

It has been suggested that *Little Women*, along with Horatio
Alger's *Bound to Rise* and Martha Finley's *Elsie Dinsmore*, are
examples of books that introduce new complexities and subtleties to what were previously clear-cut moral decisions that were
correct because they were virtuous. The historian of childhood,
Bernard Wishy, writes that "after the Civil War . . . everything
seems to intervene between the best will in the world and moral
or material victory." He points in his discussion to difficulties
that echo the burdens of the moral code: "There is still the
'happy ending' but not without young people learning how
much more life costs than their predecessors realized and how
less often and more slowly the rewards of character and piety
come." He concludes by conceding that, although the notion
still endured that "the pure and innocent could save the world,
it was increasingly feared that the world might be too much for
the pure and innocent."⁵ Alcott's recognition of this notion
explains why she places so much emphasis on the practical ne-
cessities of rationality and proper education.

These complexities of the post-Civil War world suggest the
reason Alcott's work signals the end to the traditions of the
moral tale and the domestic novel within which she was working. The earlier nineteenth-century writers of moral tales had
written heavily didactic stories of strongly virtuous children
engaging in clear-cut moral victories. Alcott alters the tradition
in several ways: she specifies concretely the obligations of the
moral code, yet she lightens the didactic tone, and she provides
more realistic details about how children look and act and
speak than earlier writers did. As a result, their burdens become
more onerous and the solutions to problems more complex.
More important, she develops youthful characterizations of

such extreme wisdom and insight that the children are capable
of redeeming the sins of their parents. In both complicating the
genre and using the children as agents of their own as well as
their parents' redemption, Alcott may be said to have left few
options for further development of the moral tale. In the case
of the domestic novel, she adopted its conventions, but changed
its protagonist to adolescent women, thus altering its message
and potential audience.

Ultimately, what follows Alcott's works are imitations, such
as Margaret Sidney Lothrop's *Five Little Peppers and How They
Grew* series, and variations, such as Laura Ingalls Wilder's *Little
House on the Prairie* series. Alcott introduces the possibility of
the heroine who operates independently in adventurous situations that are free of moral and familial constraints. It is from
this characterization that the serial novels written for and about
adolescent girls at the turn of the century are derived. In a discussion of these novels, Jane S. Smith describes the heroines
as independent and free from conventional restrictions.[6]

Although Alcott portrays no girls with such extreme independence as those that Smith describes in her article, she suggests
all the themes in her stories that the serial novelists develop:
coping with new roles and responsibilities in a changing society;
developing a sense of adventurous exploration of an interesting
world; consolidating social position; establishing independence
within domesticity; understanding the need for education and
the value of physical education; and developing a sense of female superiority. The characterizations lead to the female
sleuths of the 1930s such as Nancy Drew and the Dana girls,
who are still popular favorites today. Having created the potentially perfect child, who is capable of redeeming the adults in
her family and social circle, Alcott left little recourse for future
authors but to remove the young woman from the domestic
sphere and to allow her independent action in the world at
large—an idea that is tempting to Alcott but that she never
develops because the framework of the moral tale did not permit it.

There is a final way in which we can see that Alcott understood the practical nature of her work. That message is suggested in the concluding story of the final *Scrap-Bag* collection

—"Fancy's Friend." We originally considered "Fancy's Friend" in chapter 1 in the discussion of reservations that were held in the nineteenth century about the value of fiction for children, concluding the allegory suggests Alcott conceded that although fantasy gave pleasure to children, ultimately it had to be replaced by an acquiescence to reality. Recall that in the story Uncle Fact and Aunt Fiction are rearing their niece Fancy, who becomes enthralled with a fantasy-creation she calls Lorelei. Although Aunt Fiction points out the values that fantasy can bring, Uncle Fact disapproves and, while Aunt Fiction is away, insists that Fancy give up Lorelei, even though Lorelei has been willing to sing a little moral tale to please Uncle Fact.

Interestingly, this is the only *Scrap-Bag* story in which a man plays an important role in shaping the behavior of a child. Aunt Fiction is away on a brief trip and hence is deprived of the opportunity to participate in Fancy's decision to give up Lorelei; in contriving the scene this way Alcott also avoids any direct confrontation between Fact and Fiction. Alcott's portrayal of Fact as masculine and Fiction as feminine is consistent with nineteenth-century expectations about male and female roles and suggests Alcott's awareness of patriarchal manipulation of values and attitudes.

The allegory suggests Alcott's recognition of a larger world view than that represented in the *Scrap-Bag* stories. Uncle Fact's concern is for survival in the economic and political arena; Aunt Fiction's role is construed more narrowly to the domestic concerns of the home and is relegated to the interpretation of feeling and attitudes, to the glories of the enrichment of the personal life of the imagination. However important these latter qualities may be, thay must be superseded by a sense of fact— that which is real. The story suggests that however seriously women took the realities of the domestic sphere and insisted on the opportunities that arose therein, the world outside the home was controlled largely by men who influenced the world of women.

Originally "Fancy's Friend" was published in *Morning-Glories and Other Stories* in 1867 buried twelfth in a collection of fourteen stories. There is no evidence to suggest whether Alcott or her editor arranged the stories in the volume; if the editor

Thomas Niles was responsible, certainly he referred such an important matter to Alcott for her approval. In either circumstance the case is clear. In the *Scrap-Bag* collection, Alcott was also realistically assigning her *Scrap-Bag* stories to the category of professional writing that answered a market demand and played a practical role in the education of the child, thus giving them a place in Uncle Fact's world. The placement may be also an attempt at rationalization in that in choosing the didactic mode, Alcott gave up the opportunity to strive for truly great artistry. In writing to meet the financial responsibilities and exigencies of her family's life, she sacrificed the opportunity to produce another masterpiece that was equal to or greater than *Little Women*. She is, in fact, explaining a silence in her art similar to that of Rebecca Harding Davis after her first great work, *Life in the Iron Mills*.[7]

The story's placement suggests a final light ironic touch that indicates Alcott's understanding of the relationship of the domestic sphere to the total social, economic, and political situation. It is a recognition that the domestic sphere is essentially private and that the other is essentially public. It is a recognition that, although she is serious about the possibilities for change, represented in her phrase "promise of destiny," there is also the public world controlled largely by men that operates according to different guiding principles and values. In "Fancy's Friend" she suggests that the softer more feminine values of the traditional domestic sphere must yield to the realities of what Alcott calls Fact, to the tougher masculine values of the world at large. But the sense of loss in doing so is great enough to indicate that ultimately Alcott believes the best solution will be a joint one made by both men and women who are, if possible, operating according to the basic values of labor, love, and hope of her moral code.

The roles for women that Alcott raises in "Fancy's Friend" and indirectly in many of her other stories suggest issues similar to those being discussed today as we debate the issue of equality for women. The discussion still revolves around the distinctions of public and private roles for women. There is still a great resistance on the part of many women to accept full participation in the public sphere because they feel that in doing so they will be forced to give up the power and status that is conferred upon them in their private, traditionally domestic role. They are supported in this belief by many men who prefer the status quo. In spite of her support for women's traditional domestic roles, Alcott's *Scrap-Bag* stories suggest that she would have endorsed female participation outside of the home. She most certainly supported the right for women to vote. The certainty of change that is apparent in her stories and the need to prepare for it so that women can fulfill whatever possibilities develop suggest Alcott understood that destiny to include full participation in society.

From this study we can also see that the concerns and hopes of parents for their children are largely the same today as they were when Alcott was writing her moral tales. Parents continue to be interested in rearing their children in the best possible way, and they seek advice on how to do so, although today that advice comes more often from experts on effective parenting who operate outside of the family circle than it did in the nineteenth century. We have come to take for granted many of the causes that Alcott argues for in her stories. Although the moral tale has faded from the scene as a means of teaching children, parents still guide their children to become good or right in conduct and character by suggesting an ideal for which to strive.

NOTES

1. Nancy F. Cott, *The Bonds of Womanhood* (New Haven: Yale University Press, 1977), p. 5.

2. Thomas H. Pauly, "*Ragged Dick* and *Little Women*," *Journal of Popular Culture*, 9 (Winter 1975), 583.

3. Philip Greven, *The Protestant Temperament* (New York: Alfred A. Knopf, 1977), p. 178.

4. Bernard Wishy, *The Child and the Republic* (Philadelphia: University of Pennsylvania Press, 1972), p. 79.

5. Ibid., p. 93.

6. Jane S. Smith, "Plucky Little Ladies and Stout-Hearted Chums," *Prospects*, 3 (1977), 161.

7. Tille Olsen, *Silences* (New York: Delta/Seymour Laurence, 1978), pp. 47-118.

Appendix: The Publication Record of "Scrap-Bag" Stories*

My Boys, Etc., Aunt Jo's Scrap Bag. Boston: Roberts Brothers, 1872, 215 pp. Copyrighted 1871.

"My Boys"

The "Laddie" portion was originally published as "My Polish Boy," *The Youth's Companion*, XLI, 48 and 49 (November 26 and December 3, 1868).

"Tessa's Surprises"

Originally published in *Merry's Museum*, I, 12 (December 1868).

"Buzz"

Originally published as "My Little Friend," *Merry's Museum*, I, 2 (February 1868). Reprinted in *Sparkles for Bright Eyes* (New York: Crowell, [1879]).

"The Children's Joke"

"Dandelion"

Originally published as "The Little Boats," *Merry's Museum*, II, 4 (April 1869).

"Madam Cluck and Her Family"

Originally published in *Merry's Museum*, II, 8 (August 1869).

"A Curious Call"

Originally published in *Merry's Museum*, II, 2 (February 1869).

"Tilly's Christmas"

*Publication data were drawn from Madeleine B. Stern's "Bibliography" in *Louisa May Alcott* (Norman: University of Oklahoma Press, 1950), pp. 343-360 and Alma J. Payne's *Louisa May Alcott: A Reference Guide* (Boston: G. K. Hall and Co., 1980). Judith C. Ullom's *Louisa May Alcott: A Centennial for Little Women, An Annotated, Selected Bibliography* (Washington: Library of Congress, 1969) was also helpful.

Originally published in *Merry's Museum*, I (n.s.), 1 (January 1868). Reprinted as "The Fairy Bird," *Merry's Museum*, LXII, 4 (October 1872) and *Happy Days for Boys and Girls* (Philadelphia: Porter and Coates, [1877]).

"My Little Gentleman"

Originally published as "A Little Gentleman," *Merry's Museum*, II, 6 (June 1869).

"Back Windows"

Originally published in *Merry's Museum*, II, 1 (January 1869).

"Little Marie of Lehon"

"My May-Day Among Curious Birds and Beasts"

Originally published in *Merry's Museum*, I, 3 (March 1868). Reprinted in *Sparkles for Bright Eyes* (New York: Crowell, [1879]).

"Our Little Newsboy"

Originally published in *Merry's Museum*, I, 4 (April 1868). Reprinted in *The Youth's Companion*, XLI, 25 (June 18, 1868); in *The Christian Register*, LI, 47 (November 23, 1872); and in *Sparkles for Bright Eyes* (New York: Crowell, [1879]).

"Patty's Patchwork"

Shawl-Straps. Aunt Jo's Scrap-Bag. Vol. II. Boston: Roberts Brothers, 1872, 226 pp.

Portions of *Shawl-Straps* originally appeared in the following periodicals:

"A Dickens Day," *The Independent*, XIX, 995 (December 27, 1867).

"Women in Brittany," *The Christian Register*, LI, 1 (January 6, 1872).

"Shawl Straps," *The Christian Union*, V, 12, 13, 14, and 15 (March 13, 20, 27, and April 3, 1872).

"Pelagie's Wedding," *The Independent*, XXIV, 1227 (June 6, 1872).

Cupid and Chow-Chow, Etc., Aunt Jo's Scrap-Bag. Vol. III. Boston: Roberts Brothers, 1874, 209 pp.

"Cupid and Chow-Chow"

Originally appeared in *Hearth and Home*, IV, 20 and 21 (May 18 and 25, 1872).

"Huckleberry"

Originally appeared in *The Youth's Companion*, XLVI, 3 (January 16, 1873). Reprinted in *The Christian Register*, LII, 4 (January 25, 1873).

"Nelly's Hospital"

Originally published in *Our Young Folks*, I, 4 (April 1865). Reprinted, Washington, D.C., U.S. Sanitary Commission, 1868.

"Grandma's Team"

Originally published in *The Youth's Companion*, XLV, 48 (November 28, 1872). Reprinted in *The Christian Register*, LI, 52 (December 28, 1872).

"Fairy Pinafores"
"Mamma's Plot"
Originally published in *The Youth's Companion*, XLVI, 6
(February 6, 1873).
"Kate's Choice"
Originally published in *Hearth and Home*, IV, 2 and 3 (January
13 and 20, 1872).
"The Moss People"
"What Fanny Heard"
Originally published in *The Youth's Companion*, XLII, 19 (May 13,
1869).
"A Marine Merry-Making"
Originally published in *Merry's Museum*, II, 10 (October 1869).
My Girls, Etc., Aunt Jo's Scrap-Bag. Vol. IV. Boston: Roberts Brothers,
1878, 229 pp. Copyrighted 1877.
"My Girls"
"Lost in a London Fog"
Originally published in *The Youth's Companion*, XLVII, 15
(April 9, 1874). Reprinted in *The Christian Register*, LIII, 23
(June 6, 1874).
"The Boys' Joke, and Who Got the Best of It"
"Roses and Forget-Me-Nots"
Originally published in *St. Nicholas*, I, 5 (March 1874).
"Old Major"
Originally published in *The Youth's Companion*, XLVIII, 31
(August 5, 1875). Reprinted in *The Christian Register*, LIV, 34
(August 21, 1875).
"What the Girls Did"
Originally published in *The Youth's Companion*, XLVII, 20 (May
14, 1874). Reprinted in *The Christian Register*, LIII, 29 (July 18, 1874).
"Little Neighbors"
Originally published in *Hearth and Home*, VI, 15 and 16 (April
11 and 18, 1874).
"Marjorie's Three Gifts"
Originally published as "Marjorie's Birthday Gifts," *St. Nicholas*,
III, 3 (January 1876).
"Patty's Place"
Originally published in *Young Folks' Journal* (private enterprise),
III, 11 and 12 (January and February 1874).
"The Autobiography of an Omnibus"
A portion of this story was originally published as "Living in an
Omnibus. A True Story," in *Merry's Museum*, LIV, 4 (October
1867) and reprinted in *Merry Times for Boys and Girls* (Philadel-

phia: Porter and Coates, [1878]. The story was reprinted with
changes and title that appear in this collection in *St. Nicholas*, I,
12 (October 1874).

"Red Tulips"
   Originally published in *The Youth's Companion*, XLVIII, 8
   (February 25, 1875). Reprinted in *The Christian Register*, LIV,
   40 (October 2, 1875).

"A Happy Birthday"
   Originally published in *The Youth's Companion*, XLVII, 6
   (February 5, 1874). Reprinted in *The Christian Register*, LIII,
   10 (March 7, 1874).

Jimmy's Cruise in the Pinafore, Etc., Aunt Jo's Scrap-Bag. Vol. V. Boston:
   Roberts Brothers, 1879, 209 pp.

   "Jimmy's Cruise in the Pinafore"
      Originally published in *St. Nicholas*, VI, 12 (October 1879).

   "Two Little Travellers"
      Originally published in *St. Nicholas*, VI, 8 (June 1879).

   "A Jolly Fourth"

   "Seven Black Cats"
      Originally published in *The Youth's Companion*, XLVI, 31
      (July 31, 1873).

   "Rosa's Tale"

   "Lunch"

   "A Bright Idea"
      Originally published as "Clara's Idea" in *The Youth's Companion*,
      L, 37 (September 13, 1877).

   "How They Camped Out"

   "My Little School-Girl"
      Originally published in *The Youth's Companion*, XLVIII, 44
      (November 4, 1875). Reprinted in *The Christian Register*, LV, 6
      (February 5, 1876).

   "What A Shovel Did"
      Originally published in *The Youth's Companion*, XLVIII, 15
      (April 15, 1875).

   "Clams. A Ghost Story"
      Originally published in *The Youth's Companion*, L, 18 (May 3,
      1877).

   "Kitty's Cattle Show"

   "What Becomes of the Pins"

An Old-Fashioned Thanksgiving, Etc., Aunt Jo's Scrap-Bag. Vol. VI.
   Boston: Roberts Brothers, 1882, 234 pp.

   "An Old-Fashioned Thanksgiving"
      Originally published in *St. Nicholas*, IX, 1 (November 1881).

"How It All Happened"
Originally published in *Harper's Young People*, II, 60 (December 21, 1880).
"The Dolls' Journey from Minnesota to Maine"
"Morning-Glories"
Originally published in *Morning-Glories, and Other Stories* (Boston: Horace B. Fuller, 1868). Copyrighted December, 1867.
"Shadow-Children"
Originally published in *Morning-Glories, and Other Stories*.
"Poppy's Pranks"
Originally published in *Morning-Glories, and Other Stories*.
"What the Swallows Did"
Originally published in *Morning-Glories, and Other Stories*.
"Little Gulliver"
Originally published in *Morning-Glories, and Other Stories*.
"The Whale's Story"
Originally published in *Morning-Glories, and Other Stories*.
"A Strange Island"
Originally published in *Morning-Glories, and Other Stories*.
"Fancy's Friend"
Originally published in *Morning-Glories, and Other Stories*.
"The Rock and the Bubble," a poem that appears in the text of the story, was originally published in *The Little Pilgrim*, V, 9 (September 1858).

Bibliography

Alcott, Louisa May. *Aunt Jo's Scrap-Bag: My Boys, Etc.* Vol. I. Boston: Roberts Brothers, 1897.

———. *Aunt Jo's Scrap-Bag: Shawl-Straps.* Vol. II. Boston: Roberts Brothers, 1895.

———. *Aunt Jo's Scrap-Bag: Cupid and Chow-Chow, Etc.* Vol. III. Boston: Roberts Brothers, 1896.

———. *Aunt Jo's Scrap-Bag: My Girls, Etc.* Vol. IV. Boston: Roberts Brothers, 1892.

———. *Aunt Jo's Scrap-Bag: Jimmy's Cruise in the Pinafore, Etc.* Boston: Robert Brothers, 1896.

———. *Aunt Jo's Scrap-Bag: An Old-Fashioned Thanksgiving, Etc.* Boston: Roberts Brothers, 1897.

———. *Behind A Mask: The Unknown Thrillers of Louisa May Alcott.* Ed. and Intro. by Madeleine Stern. New York: William Morrow and Company, 1975.

———. *A Garland for Girls.* New York: Grosset and Dunlap, 1977.

———. *Jo's Boys: A Sequel to "Little Men."* Illustrated Junior Library. New York: Grosset and Dunlap, 1949.

———. *Little Men: Life at Plumfield with Jo's Boys.* New York: Collier Books, 1962.

———. *Little Women, or Meg, Jo, Beth and Amy,* Parts I and II. New York: Collier Books, 1962.

———. *Morning-Glories, and Other Stories.* New York: G. W. Carleton and Co., 1871.

———. *Rose in Bloom.* New York: Grosset and Dunlap, 1976.

———. *Plots and Counterplots: More Unknown Thrillers of Louisa May Alcott.* Ed. and Intro. by Madeleine Stern. New York: Popular Library, 1976.

――. *Work: A Story of Experience*. Intro. by Sarah Elbert. New York: Schocken Books, 1977.

Ariès, Philippe. *Centuries of Childhood: A Social History of Family Life*. Tr. Robert Baldick. New York: Vintage Books, 1962.

Baym, Nina. *Woman's Fiction: A Guide to Novels by and about Women in America, 1820-1870*. Ithaca, New York: Cornell University Press, 1978.

Bedell, Madelon. *The Alcotts: Biography of a Family*. New York: Clarkson N. Potter, Inc., 1980.

Cheney, Ednah D., ed. *Louisa May Alcott: Her Life, Letters, and Journals*. Boston: Roberts Brothers, 1890.

Child, Mrs. [Lydia Marie]. *The Mother's Book*. Family in America Series. New York: Arno Press and The New York Times, 1972.

[Child, Lydia Marie.] *Evenings in New England*. Boston: Cummings, Hilbard & Co., 1824.

Conrad, Susan. *Perish the Thought: Intellectual Women in Romantic America, 1830-1860*. New York: Oxford University Press, 1976.

Cott, Nancy F. *The Bonds of Womanhood: "Woman's Sphere" in New England, 1780-1835*. New Haven, Conn.: Yale University Press, 1977.

――. "Notes Toward an Interpretation of Antebellum Childrearing." *The Psychohistory Review*, 6 (Spring 1978), 4-20.

――. and Elizabeth H. Pleck, eds. *A Heritage of Her Own: Toward A New Social History of American Women*. New York: Simon and Schuster, 1979.

Douglas, Ann. *The Feminization of American Culture*. New York: Avon Books, 1977.

Emerson, Ralph Waldo. *The Portable Emerson*. Ed. Mark Van Doren. New York: The Viking Press, 1946.

Fass, Paula. *The Damned and the Beautiful: American Youth in the 1920s*. New York: Oxford University Press, 1977.

Fiedler, Leslie A. *Love and Death in the American Novel*. Revised Edition. New York: Stein and Day, 1975.

Gay, Carol. "The Philosopher and His Daughter: Amos Bronson Alcott and Louisa." *Essays in Literature, Western Illinois University*, 2 (1975), 181-191.

Gilbert, Sandra M. and Susan Gubar. *The Madwoman in the Attic: The Woman Writer and the Nineteenth-Century Literary Imagination*. New Haven, Conn.: Yale University Press, 1979.

Greven, Philip J., Jr. *Child-Rearing Concepts, 1626-1861: Historical Sources*, Itasca, Ill.: F. E. Peacock Publishers, Inc., 1973.

Greven, Philip. *The Protestant Temperament: Patterns of Child-Rearing, Religious Experience, and the Self in Early America.* New York: Alfred A. Knopf, 1977.

Heine, Heinrich. "Lorelei," *Lyric Poems and Ballads.* Translated by Ernst Fiese. Pittsburgh: University of Pittsburgh Press, 1968.

Hentz, Caroline Lee. *Aunt Patty's Scrap-Bag.* Philadelphia: Carey & Hart, 1846.

Hernstadt, Richard L., ed. *The Letters of A. Bronson Alcott.* Ames, Iowa: The Iowa State University Press, 1969.

James, William. *The Varieties of Religious Experience: A Study in Human Nature.* New York: Mentor Books, 1958.

Kelly, R. Gordon. "American Children's Literature: An Historiographical Review." *American Literary Realism,* 6 (Spring 1973), 89-107.

———. "Literature and the Historian." *American Quarterly,* 26 (May 1974), 141-159.

———. *Mother Was A Lady: Self and Society in Selected American Children's Periodicals, 1865-1890.* Westport, Conn.: Greenwood Press, 1974.

Kett, Joseph F. *Rites of Passage: Adolescence in America, 1790 to the Present.* New York: Basic Books, Inc., 1977.

Kuhn, Anne L. *The Mother's Role in Childhood Education: New England Concepts, 1830-1860.* New Haven: Yale University Press, 1947.

MacLeod, Anne Scott. *A Moral Tale: Children's Fiction and American Culture, 1820-1860.* Hamden, Conn.: Archon Books, 1975.

McCurry, Niki Alpert. "Concepts of Childrearing and Schooling in the March Novels of Louisa May Alcott." Ph. D. Dissertation, Northwestern University, 1976.

McIntosh, Maria J. *Evenings at Donaldson Manor: or The Christmas Guest.* New York: D. Appleton & Century, 1851.

Meyer, Donald. *The Positive Thinkers: A Study of the American Quest for Health, Wealth and Personal Power from Mary Baker Eddy to Norman Vincent Peale.* Garden City, New York: Doubleday and Company, Inc., 1965.

Morgan, Edmund S. *The Puritan Family: Religious and Domestic Relations in Seventeenth-Century New England.* New Edition, Revised and Enlarged. New York: Harper and Row, 1966.

Olsen, Tillie. *Silences.* New York: Delta/Seymour Laurence, 1978.

Pauly, Thomas H. "*Ragged Dick* and *Little Women:* Idealized Homes and Unwanted Marriages." *Journal of Popular Culture,* 9 (Winter 1975), 583-592.

Payne, Alma J. "Duty's Child: Louisa May Alcott," *American Literary*

Realism, 1870-1910, 6, no. 3 (Summer 1973), 260-261.

————. "Louisa May Alcott (1832-1888)," *American Literary Realism, 1870-1910,* 6, no. 1 (Winter 1973), 27-45.

————. *Louisa May Alcott: A Reference Guide.* Boston: G. K. Hall & Co., 1980.

Peabody, Elizabeth Palmer. *Record of a School.* New York: Arno Press and The New York Times, 1969.

Plumb, A. J. "The New World of Children in Eighteenth-Century England," *Past and Present,* 67 (May 1975), 64-95.

Ronda, Bruce Allen. "The Transcendental Child: Images and Concepts of the Child in American Transcendentalism," Dissertation, Yale University, 1975.

Saxton, Martha. *Louisa May: A Modern Biography of Louisa May Alcott.* New York: Avon Books, 1977.

Shepard, Odell, ed. *The Journals of Bronson Alcott.* Boston: Little, Brown and Company, 1938.

Shull, Martha Irene Smith. "The Novels of Louisa May Alcott as Commentary on the American Family." Dissertation, Bowling Green State University, 1975.

Sklar, Kathryn Kish. *Catherine Beecher: A Study in American Domesticity.* New Haven: Yale University Press, 1974.

Slater, Peter Gregg. *Children in the New England Mind: In Death and in Life.* Hamden, Connecticut: Archon Books, 1977.

Smith, Daniel Scott. "Family Limitation, Sexual Control, and Domestic Feminism in Victorian America." *Feminist Studies* 1 (Winter-Spring 1973), 40-57.

Smith, Jane S. "Plucky Little Ladies and Stout-Hearted Chums: Serial Novels for Girls, 1900-1920," *Prospects: An Annual of American Cultural Studies,* Ed. Jack Salzman, 3 (1977), 155-174.

Smith-Rosenburg, Carroll. "Beauty, the Beast, and the Militant Woman: A Case Study in Sex Roles and Social Stress in Jacksonian America," *American Quarterly,* 23 (1971), 562-584.

————. "The Female World of Love and Ritual: Relations Between Women In Nineteenth-Century America." *Signs: A Journal of Women in Culture and Society,* 1 (Autumn 1975), 1-29.

Stern, Madeleine B. *Louisa May Alcott.* Norman: University of Oklahoma Press, 1950.

————. "Louisa M. Alcott: An Appraisal," *New England Quarterly* 12 (December 1949), 475-498.

Strickland, Charles. "A Transcendentalist Father: The Child-rearing Practices of Bronson Alcott," *History of Childhood Quarterly,* I (Summer 1973), 4-51.

Sykes, Richard E. "American Studies and the Concept of Culture: A Theory and Method," in Robert Merideth, Ed., *American Studies: Essays on Theory and Method*. Columbus, Ohio: Charles E. Merrill Publishing Company, 1968.

Thompson, Lovell, ed. *Youth's Companion*. Boston: Houghton Mifflin, 1954.

de Tocqueville, Alexis. *Democracy in America*. Edited, Abridged, and Introduced by Andrew Hacker. New York: Washington Square Press, 1964.

Trensky, Anne Tropp. "The Bad Boy in Nineteenth-Century American Fiction," *The Georgia Review*, 27 (Winter 1973), 503-517.

———. "The Saintly Child in Nineteenth-Century American Fiction." *Prospects: An Annual of American Cultural Studies*, Ed. Jack Salzman, 1 (1975), 389-413.

Ullom, Judith C., Comp. *Louisa May Alcott: A Centennial for Little Women, An Annotated, Selected Bibliography*. Washington, D.C.: Library of Congress, 1969.

Veblen, Thorstein. *The Theory of the Leisure Class: An Economic Study of Institutions*. Intro. by C. Wright Mills. New York: New American Library, 1953.

Welter, Barbara. *Dimity Convictions: The American Woman in the Nineteenth Century*. Athens: Ohio University Press, 1976.

———. *The Woman in Question in American History*. Hinsdale, Illinois: The Dryden Press, 1973.

Wishy, Bernard. *The Child and the Republic: The Dawn of American Child Nurture*. Philadelphia: University of Pennsylvania Press, 1972.

Index

JOY MARSELLA is Assistant Professor of English at the University of Hawaii at Manoa, from which she received her Ph.D. in 1981. Her articles have appeared in *College Composition and Communication, Washington English Journal,* and *Philippine Studies.*